OPEN BORDERS

THE SCIENCE AND ETHICS OF IMMIGRATION

WRITTEN BY
BRYAN CAPLAN

ARTWORK BY
ZACH WEINERSMITH

COLOR BY
MARY CAGLE

First Second
NEW YORK

TO CORINA CAPLAN,
THE IMMIGRANT WHO
SHARES MY LIFE...

AND TO HER PARENTS,
WHO BROUGHT HER
HERE TO ME.

FOR MY GREAT-GRANDFATHER'S ONLY SISTER, PELTA WOLACH
(NÉE WINOKUR), AND HER FAMILY WHO STAYED BEHIND WHEN
HER BROTHER CAME TO AMERICA IN 1925.

TO THE BEST OF MY KNOWLEDGE, PELTA DIED IN THE LATE
'30S, AND HER HUSBAND, ICCHOK, AND ALL OF THEIR SONS
WERE MURDERED IN 1942 OR 1943 AS PART OF THE LIQUIDATION
OF BIALYSTOK'S JEWS. ONE DAUGHTER OF THEIRS, NAMED
TAUBA (OR PERHAPS TEIBEL), MARRIED A MAN NAMED MOSHE
LEV, AND THOUGH I BELIEVE THEY MADE IT ALIVE TO ISRAEL
I'VE BEEN UNABLE TO FIND INFORMATION ABOUT THEM OTHER
THAN A BRIEF MENTION IN A FAMILY RECORD AND THE
DOCUMENTS FROM YAD VASHEM.

ANY INSIGHT ABOUT THEM WOULD BE WELCOME
AND MAY BE SENT TO ZACH@SMBC-COMICS.COM.

CONTENTS

CHAPTER 1
GLOBAL APARTHEID

LIFE IS IMPROVING.

THE WORLD'S AVERAGE REAL INCOME HAS ALMOST DOUBLED OVER THE LAST TWENTY-FIVE YEARS.

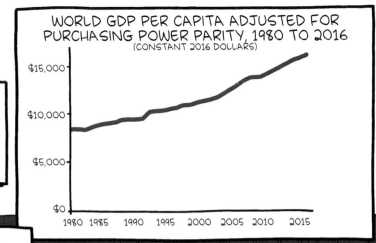

WORLD GDP PER CAPITA ADJUSTED FOR PURCHASING POWER PARITY, 1980 TO 2016
(CONSTANT 2016 DOLLARS)

AND INCOMES OF THE GLOBAL POOR HAVE GROWN ESPECIALLY QUICKLY.

THE GLOBAL POVERTY RATE HAS FALLEN BY OVER TWO-THIRDS. TOTAL PEOPLE IN POVERTY HAS FALLEN BY MORE THAN HALF, DESPITE RISING POPULATION.

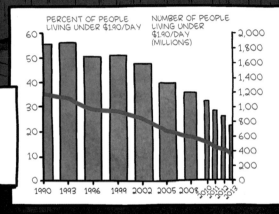

I'M BRYAN CAPLAN, ECONOMICS PROFESSOR AT GEORGE MASON UNIVERSITY.

LIKE 99% OF ECONOMISTS, I'M THRILLED TO SEE GLOBAL PROSPERITY BLOSSOM AND POVERTY WITHER RIGHT BEFORE MY EYES.

BUT I'M ALSO DISAPPOINTED. DESPITE GREAT PROGRESS, TWO FACTS REMAIN:

FIRST, LIFE IS SWEET IN RICH COUNTRIES, BUT HARSH IN POOR COUNTRIES.

SECOND, AT CURRENT RATES, POOR COUNTRIES WON'T BE RICH FOR MANY DECADES.

WHICH BRINGS US TO THE HUNDRED-*TRILLION*-DOLLAR QUESTION:

NOT CONVINCED.? JUST LOOK AT THE PRICES HUMAN SMUGGLERS CHARGE TO HELP MIGRANTS JUMP THE BORDER.

"COYOTES" ASK ABOUT $4,000 TO CROSS FROM MEXICO TO THE U.S. THAT'S SEVERAL *YEARS*' INCOME FOR A RURAL MEXICAN FARM WORKER.

AND PAYING THE FEE HARDLY ENSURES ADMISSION. HALF OF ALL MEXICANS WHO ENTER THE U.S. ILLEGALLY GET CAUGHT AND SENT HOME.

SMUGGLING FEES FOR MORE REMOTE LOCATIONS ARE EVEN HIGHER. $50,000 FROM CHINA!

YEARS OF TOIL DOWN THE DRAIN.

BOTTOM LINE: IMMIGRATION LAWS "WORK" IN THE SENSE THAT THEY DRASTICALLY REDUCE IMMIGRATION.

14

OPEN BORDERS?

HERE'S HOW PHILOSOPHER MICHAEL HUEMER EXPLAINS IT IN HIS "STARVING MARVIN" HYPOTHETICAL.

"MARVIN IS IN DESPERATE NEED OF FOOD. PERHAPS SOMEONE HAS STOLEN HIS FOOD OR PERHAPS A NATURAL DISASTER DESTROYED HIS CROPS. WHATEVER THE REASON, MARVIN IS IN DANGER OF STARVATION."

"FORTUNATELY, HE HAS A PLAN TO REMEDY THE PROBLEM: HE WILL WALK TO THE LOCAL MARKETPLACE, WHERE HE WILL BUY BREAD."

FREEZE, MARVIN!

"ANOTHER INDIVIDUAL, SAM, IS AWARE OF ALL THIS AND IS WATCHING MARVIN. SAM DECIDES TO DETAIN MARVIN ON HIS WAY TO THE MARKETPLACE, FORCIBLY PREVENTING HIM FROM REACHING IT."

"AS A RESULT, MARVIN RETURNS HOME EMPTY-HANDED, WHERE HE DIES OF STARVATION."

"WHAT IS THE PROPER ASSESSMENT OF SAM'S ACTIONS?"

"SAM'S BEHAVIOR IN THIS SCENARIO WAS BOTH EXTREMELY HARMFUL TO MARVIN, AND A SEVERE VIOLATION OF MARVIN'S RIGHTS. INDEED, IF MARVIN'S DEATH WAS REASONABLY FORESEEABLE, THEN SAM'S ACT WAS AN ACT OF *MURDER*."

HUEMER'S POINT REMAINS THE SAME IF THE HARM IS MILDER. IF MARVIN GETS MALNUTRITION INSTEAD OF DYING, SAM STILL DID HIM A GRAVE WRONG.

NOW, WHAT DOES THE MARVIN-SAM SAGA HAVE TO DO WITH IMMIGRATION RESTRICTION?

EVERYTHING!

WHEN GOVERNMENTS RESTRICT IMMIGRATION, THEY AREN'T SIMPLY REFUSING TO HELP THE GLOBAL POOR.

SORRY, I GAVE AT THE CAPITOL.

THEY'RE BARRING TRADE BETWEEN NATIVES AND FOREIGNERS—TRADE THAT LETS THE GLOBAL POOR WORK THEIR WAY OUT OF POVERTY.

QUESTION:

IF THIS IS WRONG FOR SAM, WHY ISN'T IT WRONG FOR *UNCLE* SAM?

THE "GOLDEN GOOSE" RESPONSE WOULD BE FAR MORE COMPELLING IF THE UNITED STATES DIDN'T *HAVE* VIRTUALLY OPEN BORDERS UNTIL THE 1920S.

WITH INFAMOUS EXCEPTIONS...

ANYONE COULD COME.

A MIGHTY WOMAN WITH A TORCH, WHOSE FLAME IS THE IMPRISONED LIGHTNING, AND HER NAME MOTHER OF EXILES. FROM HER BEACON-HAND GLOWS WORLD-WIDE WELCOME...

"GIVE ME YOUR TIRED, YOUR POOR, YOUR HUDDLED MASSES YEARNING TO BREATHE FREE, THE WRETCHED REFUSE OF YOUR TEEMING SHORE. SEND THESE, THE HOMELESS, TEMPEST-TOST TO ME, I LIFT MY LAMP BESIDE THE GOLDEN DOOR!"

*EMMA LAZARUS, "THE NEW COLOSSUS"

DESPITE OPPOSITION THAT MUST BE SEEN TO BE BELIEVED...

AMERICA'S GOLDEN GOOSE DIDN'T JUST SURVIVE THE OPEN BORDERS ERA.

IT THRIVED.

THE U.S.A. BECAME THE WORLD'S RICHEST AND MOST POWERFUL NATION.

WHEN THE U.S. DECISIVELY TURNED AGAINST OPEN BORDERS IN THE 1920S, THE RATIONALE WAS FLIMSY AT BEST.

OUR NORDIC RACE IS IMPERILED BY IMMIGRANTS OF INFERIOR STOCK!

CAN OUR REPUBLIC LONG ENDURE THIS FLOOD OF...

SOUTHERN EUROPEANS?

EASTERN EUROPEANS?

AND JEWS?!

THIS IS NOT SORDID SPECULATION, BUT HISTORICAL FACT.

BY BASING NATIONS' IMMIGRATION QUOTAS ON THE CENSUS OF 1890—RIGHT BEFORE THE DAWN OF HIGH IMMIGRATION FROM SOUTHERN AND EASTERN EUROPE.

THE KEY LEGISLATION—THE 1924 IMMIGRATION ACT—CONSCIOUSLY TURNED BACK THE COUNTRY'S DEMOGRAPHIC CLOCK...

WHILE WE'RE AT IT, LET'S EXCLUDE ASIANS ALTOGETHER!

CAPITAL IDEA!

AFTER THE NAZIS GAVE RACISM A REALLY BAD NAME, THE 1924 ACT FELL INTO DISFAVOR.

UN-NORDIC!

UN-AMERICAN!

UN-THINKABLE!

THE 1965 IMMIGRATION ACT LIBERALIZED NATIONAL ORIGINS QUOTAS, ALLOWING THE DIVERSE IMMIGRATION WE'VE SEEN SINCE.

EVEN NORDICS MAKE MISTAKES.

YET DESPITE THE UGLY ORIGINS OF IMMIGRATION RESTRICTIONS, THE FACT REMAINS: MIGRATION HAS BEEN TIGHTLY REGULATED FOR NEARLY A CENTURY.

WHAT ON EARTH WOULD HAPPEN IF OPEN BORDERS WERE REINSTATED?

CRITICS PREDICT DISASTER.

SO, WHILE THERE'S A MORAL PRESUMPTION IN FAVOR OF IMMIGRATION...

AND AN AWE-INSPIRING HISTORICAL TRACK RECORD...

WE STILL NEED TO LOOK BEFORE WE LEAP.

DO THE NIGHTMARE SCENARIOS HOLD WATER?

ARE THEY AT LEAST SCARY ENOUGH TO WARRANT GREAT CAUTION?

OR WAS THE END OF OPEN BORDERS A TRAGIC MISTAKE?

A MISTAKE WE CAN, SHOULD, AND *MUST* AMEND?

CHAPTER 2

TRILLION-DOLLAR BILLS ON THE SIDEWALK

THE SECRET OF MASS CONSUMPTION...

IS MASS PRODUCTION.

BUY 1, GET 2,718 FREE!

14000 lbs. OATMEAL

WHILE PROGRESS ALWAYS HURTS SOMEONE...

SIGH TIME TO FIND A NEW LINE OF WORK.

BEEP BEEP!

VROOOM!

CONSUMERS' LIVING STANDARDS RISE WHEN WORKERS PRODUCE MORE STUFF.

WHEN WORKERS PRODUCE *VASTLY* MORE STUFF, ALMOST *EVERYONE* ENDS UP BETTER OFF.

BEFORE THE INDUSTRIAL REVOLUTION, EVEN THE RICHEST KINGS LIVED WITHOUT REFRIGERATION, ANTIBIOTICS, RUNNING WATER, AIRPLANES, AND INTERNET.

IT'S GOOD TO BE THE KING, BUT A DENTAL PLAN WOULD BE NICE.

WELCOMING ANTARCTICANS ISN'T JUST THE DECENT THING TO DO.

IT'S ALSO THE *SMART* THING TO DO. ENRICHING THE ANTARCTICANS ENRICHES HUMANITY. ENRICHING HUMANITY ENRICHES *US*.

WHAT DOES THIS THOUGHT EXPERIMENT HAVE TO DO WITH IMMIGRATION?

PLENTY!

ECONOMICALLY SPEAKING, MOST OF THE WORLD IS LIKE ANTARCTICA: INHOSPITABLE FOR WEALTH CREATION.

HOW PRODUCTIVE WOULD *YOU* BE IN HAITI?

TRUE, LOW-SKILLED IMMIGRANTS TEND TO BE... LOW SKILLED, EVEN COMPARED TO, SAY, NATIVE HIGH SCHOOL DROPOUTS.

I CAN SCULPT ICE?

BUT EVEN LOW-SKILLED WORKERS ARE VASTLY MORE PRODUCTIVE IN THE FIRST WORLD THAN AT HOME.

HOW MUCH MORE PRODUCTIVE? ECONOMIST MICHAEL CLEMENS HAS DONE THE MATH.

ECONOMISTS OFTEN MEASURE WHY, SAY, MEN EARN MORE THAN WOMEN. STANDARD STATISTICAL METHOD: SEE HOW MUCH THE OBSERVED PAY GAP SHRINKS IF YOU COMPARE MALE AND FEMALE WORKERS WITH *IDENTICAL* EDUCATION, JOB EXPERIENCE, ETC.

IN "THE PLACE PREMIUM," MY COAUTHORS AND I USE THE SAME STATISTICAL METHOD TO QUANTIFY WHY PEOPLE IN THE U.S. EARN MORE THAN PEOPLE IN THE THIRD WORLD.

U.S.A.

WE COMPARE WORKERS WITH DIFFERENT COUNTRIES OF *RESIDENCE*, BUT IDENTICAL SKILLS AND COUNTRY OF *BIRTH*.

MEXICO

THE RESULTS ARE STAGGERING.

WAGE MULTIPLIER FROM MOVING TO U.S.

MEXICO   INDIA   HAITI   EGYPT   NIGERIA

MOVING THE AVERAGE THIRD-WORLDER TO THE U.S. RAISES WAGES ABOUT 400%. WHILE U.S. WORKERS ARE PLAINLY MORE SKILLED THAN THIRD-WORLD WORKERS, 60–70% OF THE GLOBAL PAY GAP STEMS FROM *WHERE* YOU ARE, NOT *WHO* YOU ARE.

THE POORER HIS COUNTRY OF BIRTH, THE MORE A MIGRANT GAINS. LEAVING NIGERIA OR HAITI INCREASES EARNINGS ABOUT *TEN FOLD*.

THE REASON ISN'T THAT U.S. BOSSES ARE NICE WHILE NIGERIAN AND HAITIAN BOSSES ARE MEAN.

ALL BOSSES WANT TO MAKE MONEY, BUT THEY COMPETE.

IF THEY PAY THEIR WORKERS LESS THAN THEY'RE WORTH, ANOTHER EMPLOYER WILL PROFIT...

...BY PAYING THEM TO JUMP SHIP!

AND BOSSES PAY MORE IN THE U.S. THAN NIGERIA OR HAITI BECAUSE NIGERIAN AND HAITIAN WORKERS ARE MORE *PRODUCTIVE* HERE THAN AT HOME.

SO WHAT WOULD HAPPEN IN AN OPEN-BORDERS WORLD WHERE *ANYONE* COULD TAKE A JOB *ANYWHERE?*

CLEMENS TACKLES THIS QUESTION IN HIS MOST FAMOUS PAPER, "ECONOMICS AND EMIGRATION: TRILLION-DOLLAR BILLS ON THE SIDEWALK?"

THE IDEA THAT IMMIGRATION CAUSES POVERTY IS AS MISGUIDED AS THE IDEA THAT TECHNOLOGY CAUSES POVERTY.

IF ANYONE COULD TAKE A JOB ANYWHERE, ESTIMATED GAINS RANGE FROM 50 TO 150% OF GROSS WORLD PRODUCT.

THAT'S ANYWHERE FROM A "PESSIMISTIC" SCENARIO WHERE OPEN BORDERS GIVES HUMANITY AN EXTRA *HALF PLANET* OF WEALTH A YEAR...

TO AN "OPTIMISTIC" SCENARIO WHERE OPEN BORDERS GIVES HUMANITY AN EXTRA ONE AND A HALF PLANETS OF WEALTH EVERY YEAR*!!!*

BUT HOW DOES THIS TRILLIONAIRE'S PIE OF WEALTH GET SLICED.?

IMMIGRANTS—ESPECIALLY LOW-SKILLED IMMIGRANTS—GAIN TREMENDOUSLY. OPEN BORDERS LETS THE GLOBAL POOR LEGALLY ENJOY GLOBAL OPPORTUNITY.

BUT IMMIGRANTS ARE FAR FROM THE ONLY BENEFICIARIES. NATIVES CONSUME THE EXTRA RICHES IMMIGRANTS PRODUCE.

CLEAR GAINERS INCLUDE REAL-ESTATE OWNERS...

RETIREES...

WORKING MOMS...

AND ANYONE WHO WORKS IN CONSTRUCTION.

LOTS OF IMMIGRANTS MEANS LOTS OF NEW HOMES, OFFICES, AND FACTORIES!

BUT DOESN'T SUPPLY AND DEMAND *ENSURE* NATIVE WORKERS LOSE? NO, BECAUSE THERE ARE *MANY* KINDS OF LABOR.

EFFECT OF IMMIGRANT *COMPETITORS*

OLD SUPPLY   NEW SUPPLY

WAGES

DEMAND

WAGES FALL!

EMPLOYMENT

EFFECT OF IMMIGRANT *CUSTOMERS*

OLD DEMAND   NEW DEMAND

WAGES

SUPPLY

WAGES RISE!

EMPLOYMENT

TRUE, IMMIGRANTS WHO *SELL* WHAT YOU SELL HURT YOU BY INCREASING LABOR *SUPPLY.*

BUT IMMIGRANTS WHO *BUY* WHAT YOU SELL HELP YOU BY INCREASING LABOR *DEMAND!*

REMEMBER: EVEN "LOW-SKILLED" AMERICANS ARE HIGH SKILLED BY WORLD STANDARDS.

THEY'RE LITERATE, FLUENT IN ENGLISH, AND KNOW THE MODERN WORLD.

THEY'LL NORMALLY BE MANAGING AND TRAINING NEW ARRIVALS, NOT COMPETING WITH THEM!

NOT CONVINCED? I CAN'T TELL YOU HOW MANY TIMES PEOPLE HAVE TOLD ME...

THAT'S REAL EASY FOR A PROFESSOR TO SAY!

YOU'VE GOT NOTHING TO WORRY ABOUT!

WRONG. DUE TO KEY IMMIGRATION LOOPHOLES, PROFESSORS LIKE ME *ALREADY* FACE NEAR-OPEN BORDERS!

Festival of Obscure Academic Quibbles '19

EVER NOTICE HOW MANY COLLEGE PROFESSORS HAVE ACCENTS? THAT'S BECAUSE RESEARCH UNIVERSITIES ARE ALMOST TOTALLY FREE TO HIRE FACULTY FROM ANY COUNTRY ON EARTH.

SINCE IMMIGRATION INCREASES THE NUMBER OF PROFESSORS FAR MORE THAN IT INCREASES THE NUMBER OF STUDENTS, MY CAREER HAS SUFFERED.

A FOREIGNER NOW OCCUPIES THE HARVARD OFFICE THAT "RIGHTLY" BELONGS TO ME!

OF COURSE, MANY OF THESE IMMIGRANT PROFESSORS ARE MY FRIENDS. IT'S NOT ALL DOLLARS AND CENTS.

BUT FRIENDSHIP ASIDE, MY GAINS FROM IMMIGRATION FAR EXCEED MY LOSSES!

BUT WON'T ALL THESE LOW-SKILLED IMMIGRANTS DEPRESS OUR COUNTRY'S AVERAGE STANDARD OF LIVING?

ALMOST CERTAINLY, BUT THERE'S NO NEED TO WORRY. YOUR FEARS REST ON THE DREADED...

ARITHMETIC FALLACY!

IMAGINE YOU'RE IN A ROOM FULL OF NBA PLAYERS.

AVERAGE HEIGHT: 6'7".

SUDDENLY, A CLASS OF PRESCHOOLERS BURSTS INTO THE ROOM. AS A MATTER OF ARITHMETIC, THE ROOM'S AVERAGE HEIGHT PLUMMETS TO 4'10". WOULD ANYONE SENSIBLE RESPOND...

OH NO!

WE'RE SHRINKING!

OF COURSE NOT. PRESCHOOLERS DON'T MAKE NBA PLAYERS SHORTER.

THE LESSON: WHEN THE MAKEUP OF THE POPULATION IS CHANGING, AVERAGES ARE DEEPLY MISLEADING. THE AVERAGE CAN EASILY FALL, EVEN THOUGH EVERYONE IS BETTER OFF!

AND THAT'S THE CRUX OF THE ECONOMIC CASE FOR OPEN BORDERS:
WE SHOULD FOCUS ON INDIVIDUALS, NOT AVERAGES. IF, FOR EXAMPLE,
THE WORLD OF TODAY LOOKS LIKE THIS...

AVERAGE NATIVE INCOME:
$50,000

AVERAGE FOREIGN INCOME:
$5,000

THEN THE WORLD OF OPEN BORDERS
WOULD LOOK LIKE THIS...

AVERAGE NATIVE
INCOME:
$60,000

AVERAGE FOREIGN
INCOME:
$20,000

AVERAGE COMBINED
INCOME:
$40,000

IF YOU SEE THESE NUMBERS AND SAY, "THE WORLD
OF OPEN BORDERS IS ECONOMICALLY INFERIOR,"
YOU ARE COMMITTING THE ARITHMETIC FALLACY.

WHAT WOULD OPEN BORDERS EVEN LOOK LIKE? IS IT REALLY PHYSICALLY POSSIBLE FOR MIGRATION TO MAKE HUMANITY TRILLIONS OF DOLLARS RICHER?

THE CLOSEST MODERN PARALLEL IS THE MASSIVE MIGRATION-FUELED GROWTH *WITHIN* CHINA AND INDIA OVER THE LAST FEW DECADES.

IN 1976, CHINA'S GDP WAS A WRETCHED $504 BILLION; INDIA'S JUST $348 BILLION.

NOW, CHINA EXCEEDS $10 TRILLION. INDIA, $2 TRILLION.

HOW DOES THIS PROSPERITY EXPLOSION HAPPEN? MARKET REFORMS GOT THE BALL ROLLING.

CAPITALIST ROAD

BUT THE BALL COULDN'T HAVE ROLLED VERY FAR IF HUNDREDS OF MILLIONS OF FARMERS HADN'T MOVED TO CITIES TO TAKE ADVANTAGE OF NEW OPPORTUNITIES.

CHINESE AND INDIAN CITIES DIDN'T JUST GROW OVER THE LAST FOUR DECADES; THEY MULTIPLIED.

MIGRANTS MAKE PROSPERITY. YOU CAN SEE IT FROM SPACE!

OPEN BORDERS WOULD BE AN UPSCALE, PLUS-SIZE VERSION OF CHINA'S AND INDIA'S ECONOMIC MIRACLES.

HUNDREDS OF MILLIONS WOULD RELOCATE—MOSTLY TO RICHER COUNTRIES!

NEW CITIES WOULD POP UP ALL OVER THE MAP!

Welcome to Startup, WYOMING

DYING FIRST-WORLD CITIES WOULD REVIVE!

NEW CITIES PACKED WITH NEW HOUSING, NEW BUSINESSES, NEW LIVES...

AND TONS OF NEW PROBLEMS.

THE RIGHT QUESTION TO ASK IS NEVER, "WILL IT BE PERFECT?"

BUT, "WILL IT BE BETTER THAN THE ALTERNATIVE?"

AND, ECONOMICALLY SPEAKING, OPEN BORDERS IS *TRILLIONS* OF DOLLARS A YEAR BETTER THAN THE ALTERNATIVE.

EVEN FANS OF IMMIGRATION WORRY OPEN BORDERS WILL LEAD TO "SWAMPING"—AN INFLUX OF MIGRANTS MORE MASSIVE THAN ANY COUNTRY CAN HANDLE.

BUT TRANSPORTATION ALONE IS A MAJOR BOTTLENECK...

AND PLENTY OF MIGRANTS WILL WAIT UNTIL THEY CAN LINE UP JOBS AND HOUSING. THIS, TOO, ADDS YEARS TO THE TRANSITION.

HISTORY TELLS US THE FIRST-MOVERS WILL BE RELATIVES AND FRIENDS OF EXISTING MIGRANTS...

WITH RELATIVES AND FRIENDS EAGER TO HELP THEM GET ON THEIR FEET.

FROM THERE, IMMIGRATION WILL *GRADUALLY* SNOWBALL. WHY GRADUALLY?

BECAUSE MIGRANTS CRAVE THEIR COUNTRYMEN'S COMPANY. CHINESE MIGRANTS, FOR EXAMPLE, PREFER DESTINATIONS WITH LARGE CHINESE POPULATIONS.

ROCKET SCIENCE *AND* KUNG PAO CHICKEN?

YOU'RE THE ONE WHO WANTED TO EXCLUDE THEM!

AS A RESULT, MIGRATION IS SLOW TO START, BUT FEEDS ON ITSELF. RESEARCHERS CALL THIS "DIASPORA DYNAMICS."

PUERTO RICAN MIGRATION TO THE U.S. IS A TEXTBOOK CASE.

Greetings from San Juan

IN 1902, U.S. IMMIGRATION OFFICIALS TRIED TO DEPORT PUERTO RICAN MIGRANT ISABEL GONZÁLEZ.

IN GONZALES V. WILLIAMS, THE U.S. SUPREME COURT MISSPELLED HER NAME BUT RULED IN HER FAVOR. PUERTO RICANS WERE *NOT* "ALIENS," AND WERE THEREFORE ENTITLED TO LIVE HERE. IN EFFECT, THE COURT DECLARED...

¡Bienvenidos!

OPEN BORDERS WITH PUERTO RICO!

WHAT HAPPENED? VERY LITTLE—AT FIRST.

OPEN

FROM 1900–1910, ABOUT 2,000 PUERTO RICANS CAME.

THE MORE PUERTO RICANS WHO CAME, HOWEVER, THE MORE PUERTO RICANS *WANTED* TO COME.

PUERTO RICO'S NET EMIGRATION (1900-2000)

UNTIL THE '70S, ALMOST ALL WENT TO NEW YORK, NOT FLORIDA. COMMUNITY OUTWEIGHS CLIMATE!

A CENTURY AFTER GONZALES V. WILLIAMS, MOST PUERTO RICANS FINALLY LIVE STATESIDE.

DIASPORA DYNAMICS!

IN ANY CASE, WE SHOULDN'T FOCUS ON "WHAT'S GOOD FOR COUNTRIES." WE SHOULD FOCUS ON WHAT'S GOOD FOR *PEOPLE*.

THINK ABOUT YOUR CLASSIC GHOST TOWN. SAD, RIGHT?

WHAT WOULD HAPPEN, THOUGH, IF PEOPLE WERE FORBIDDEN TO LEAVE GHOST TOWNS?

ECONOMIST LANT PRITCHETT SPELLS IT OUT:

THEN YOU GET SOMETHING MUCH WORSE...

A ZOMBIE ECONOMY!!!

LARGE REGIONAL FALLS IN LABOR DEMAND ARE A FACT OF LIFE.

FROM 1930–1990, AS U.S. POPULATION DOUBLED, VAST REGIONS LOST POPULATION. THE 902 SLOWEST-GROWING COUNTIES— TOTAL AREA LARGER THAN MEXICO— *LOST* 28% OF THEIR POPULATION.

50

CHAPTER 3

THE NATIVE'S BURDEN?

MARKETS ARE EVERYWHERE, BUT TRULY FREE MARKET ECONOMIES SIMPLY DON'T EXIST. EVERY GOVERNMENT ON EARTH FUNDS A VAST ARRAY OF SERVICES AND SOCIAL PROGRAMS.

MILITARY

ANOTHER ONE?

MEDICINE

PENSIONS

SCHOOLS

$$a^n + b^n = c^n$$

ROADS

WELFARE

EVERY GOVERNMENT ON EARTH FUNDS THESE PROGRAMS WITH HEFTY TAXATION.

INFAMOUS CRIMINAL WILLIE SUTTON SUPPOSEDLY SAID HE ROBBED BANKS BECAUSE...

THAT'S WHERE THE MONEY IS!

GOVERNMENTS USUALLY TARGET THE RICH FOR THE SAME REASON.

ALL THIS STRONGLY ARGUES IN FAVOR OF *HIGH*-SKILL IMMIGRATION.

SINCE HIGH-SKILL IMMIGRANTS EARN BIG BUCKS, THEY'RE CLEAR-CUT NET TAXPAYERS—PEOPLE WHOSE TAX BILL EXCEEDS THE COST OF THE GOVERNMENT SERVICES THEY CONSUME.

THE ESSENCE OF OPEN BORDERS, HOWEVER, IS TO WELCOME IMMIGRANTS OF ALL SKILL LEVELS. AND FRANKLY, MOST WOULD-BE IMMIGRANTS ARE LOW SKILL.

GIVEN FINANCIAL REALITIES, SUCH IMMIGRANTS ARE CONCEIVABLY A BIG BURDEN ON NATIVES.

FISCAL FEARS MAKE SOME OF IMMIGRATION'S SMARTEST FRIENDS REJECT OPEN BORDERS...

Milton Friedman

"YOU CANNOT SIMULTANEOUSLY HAVE FREE IMMIGRATION AND A WELFARE STATE."

Nobel Prize

Immigration Road Map
Step 1. Fix Education
Step 2. Stop Corruption
Step 3. Switch to Flat Tax
...
Step 463. Open Borders!

...OR AT LEAST TREAT OPEN BORDERS AS THE LAST STEP IN A UTOPIAN MANIFESTO.

BUT, ON REFLECTION, IMMIGRATION'S FISCAL BURDEN IS SUBTLER THAN IT LOOKS.

FIRST AND FOREMOST, MANY GOVERNMENT SERVICES ARE "NON-RIVAL."

MEANING: WHEN POPULATION RISES, THEIR *TOTAL* COST STAYS THE SAME.

NATIONAL DEFENSE IS THE CLASSIC CASE. THE U.S. MILITARY CAN DEFEND 500 MILLION AMERICANS JUST AS EASILY AS 100 MILLION AMERICANS.

IF THERE WERE ANOTHER BABY BOOM, NO ONE WOULD SAY, "WE NEED MORE NUKES TO DEFEND OUR NEW BABIES."

HENCE: EACH IMMIGRANT WHO PAYS A PENNY OF TAXES LIGHTENS THE FISCAL BURDEN OF THE MILITARY ON EVERYONE WHO'S ALREADY HERE.

THIS IS EVEN CLEARER FOR GOVERNMENT DEBT. IF SCOTLAND LEAVES BRITAIN WITHOUT TAKING ITS SHARE OF BRITAIN'S DEBT, DEBT PER REMAINING BRITON SKYROCKETS.

DOES THE DEBT SAY "SCOTLAND" ON IT? THEN SCOTLAND'S NOT PAYIN' IT!

IMMIGRATION IS LIKE SECESSION IN REVERSE: NEW TAXPAYERS HELP SHOULDER THE TAB EARLIER RESIDENTS ALREADY RACKED UP.

COMPARED TO NATIVES, IMMIGRANTS ARE A LOT LESS LIKELY TO BE...

RETIREMENT AGE...

OR SCHOOL AGE.

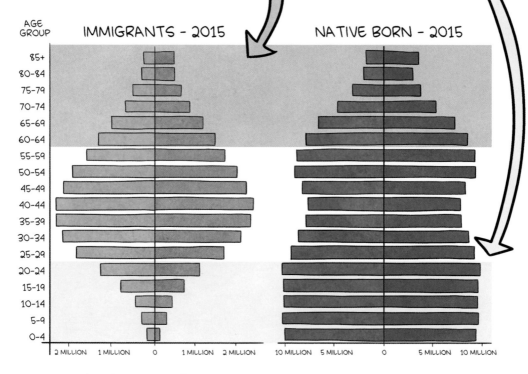

AGE GROUP

IMMIGRANTS - 2015

NATIVE BORN - 2015

85+	
80-84	
75-79	
70-74	
65-69	
60-64	
55-59	
50-54	
45-49	
40-44	
35-39	
30-34	
25-29	
20-24	
15-19	
10-14	
5-9	
0-4	

2 MILLION   1 MILLION   0   1 MILLION   2 MILLION

10 MILLION   5 MILLION   0   5 MILLION   10 MILLION

MALE   FEMALE

MALE   FEMALE

TOTAL U.S. IMMIGRANT POPULATION: 43,290,400

TOTAL U.S. NATIVE POPULATION: 278,128,400

AS A RESULT, EVEN LOW-SKILLED IMMIGRANTS ARE A LIGHTER "BURDEN" THAN YOU'D THINK.

U.S. TAXPAYERS PAY LITTLE OR NOTHING FOR A WORKING-AGE IMMIGRANT'S EDUCATION.

AVERAGE K-12 COST: $12,000 PER YEAR

TRUE, PLENTY OF IMMIGRANTS HAVE KIDS—AND STATISTICIANS COUNT ALL U.S.-BORN KIDS AS "NATIVES." BUT THE SAVINGS ARE NO GENERATIONAL TRICKERY.

PICTURE A FAMILY OF THREE NATIVES. LET'S COUNT HOW MANY PEOPLE U.S. TAXPAYERS PAID TO EDUCATE.

THAT'S RIGHT: THREE.

NOW PICTURE A FAMILY OF THREE IMMIGRANTS. HOW MANY PEOPLE DID U.S. TAXPAYERS PAY TO EDUCATE?

ONLY ONE— A BARGAIN IN ANY LANGUAGE!

AND WHILE WORKING-AGE IMMIGRANTS WILL EVENTUALLY BE ELIGIBLE FOR OLD-AGE BENEFITS...

...THE MATH STILL WORKS IN TAXPAYERS' FAVOR.

PROGRAMS LIKE SOCIAL SECURITY AND MEDICARE ARE KIND OF LIKE PYRAMID SCHEMES. THEY'RE ONLY AFFORDABLE AS LONG AS WE HAVE LOTS OF YOUNG TAXPAYERS AROUND TO SUPPORT OUR RETIREES.

RETIREES

WORKERS

RETIREES

WORKERS

IF OUR POPULATION GETS OLD ENOUGH, THE PYRAMID COLLAPSES.

CONTINUOUSLY ADMITTING LOTS OF WORKING-AGE IMMIGRANTS FATTENS THE BASE OF THE AGE PYRAMID, ALLOWING HIGHER BENEFITS WITH LOWER TAXES.

RETIREES

WORKERS

THIS 2016 REPORT FROM THE NATIONAL ACADEMY OF SCIENCES THOROUGHLY REVIEWS DECADES OF RESEARCH, THEN METICULOUSLY ESTIMATES IMMIGRATION'S *OVERALL, LONG-RUN* FISCAL EFFECT.

TAKE MY WIFE, WHO LEFT COMMUNIST ROMANIA WHEN SHE WAS SEVEN YEARS OLD.

BUNĂ ZIUA AMERICA!

AS A CHILD, SHE WENT TO CATHOLIC SCHOOL, SO SHE INITIALLY COST U.S. TAXPAYERS VERY LITTLE.

JESUS, MARY, AND JOSEPH! LEARNING ENGLISH IS EASY WHEN YOU'RE SEVEN!

BUT CALIFORNIA SUBSIDIZED HER COLLEGE EDUCATION.

AMERICA IS THE WORST!

YOU GUYS NEED TO GET OUT MORE.

AND NEW JERSEY SUBSIDIZED HER LAW SCHOOL.

HABEAS CORPUS!

ONCE SHE BECAME A CORPORATE LAWYER, SHE STARTED PAYING TAXES BY THE BOATLOAD.

AT LEAST UNCLE SAM LETS ME *KEEP* A BOATLOAD!

BUT, ONE DAY, SHE'LL GET SOCIAL SECURITY AND MEDICARE.

GRANDMA, YOU LIVED UNDER *COMMUNISM?*

IF YOU CALL THAT LIVING!

AND SINCE WE'VE GOT FOUR KIDS, THE FISCAL "CIRCLE OF LIFE" IS ALREADY REBOOTING!

SMILE, KIDS. YOU'RE IN AMERICA!

WHAT'S MY WIFE'S *OVERALL, LONG-RUN* FISCAL EFFECT? OR ANY IMMIGRANT'S? TO FIND OUT, WE HAVE TO CALCULATE WHAT ACCOUNTANTS CALL THEIR NPV, OR...

NET PRE$ENT VALUE!

$$NPV = T_{2019} + \frac{T_{2020}}{(1+r)} + \frac{T_{2021}}{(1+r)^2} + \frac{T_{2022}}{(1+r)^3} + \ldots = \sum_{n=2019}^{\infty} \frac{T_n}{(1+r)^{n-2019}}$$

where $T_n = (\$ \text{ of Taxes} - \$ \text{ of services in year } n)$
$r = \text{Interest rate}$

THE MATH IS COMPLEX, BECAUSE THE LONGER THE GOVERNMENT WAITS TO RECEIVE TAXES OR PAY FOR SERVICES, THE LOWER THEIR ACCOUNTING COST.

AN IMMIGRANT WITH AN NPV GREATER THAN $0 IS AN ASSET FOR TAXPAYERS. THE BIGGER THE NUMBER, THE BIGGER THE ASSET.

AN IMMIGRANT WITH AN NPV LESS THAN $0 IS A LIABILITY FOR TAXPAYERS. THE BIGGER THE NUMBER, THE BIGGER THE LIABILITY.

WHAT DOES THE NATIONAL ACADEMY OF SCIENCES REPORT CONCLUDE.?

FIRST, THE *OVERALL, LONG-RUN* FISCAL EFFECT OF EXISTING IMMIGRANTS IS *POSITIVE*. $58,000 PER IMMIGRANT.

$58K

SECOND, THE *OVERALL, LONG-RUN* FISCAL EFFECT OF *NEW* IMMIGRANTS IS EVEN HIGHER: $259,000 PER IMMIGRANT!

$259K

THE NUMBERS LOOK EVEN BETTER IF YOU ASSUME THE U.S. EVENTUALLY GETS ITS BUDGET DEFICIT UNDER CONTROL.

$279,000 PER NEW IMMIGRANT!

$279K

$73,000 PER IMMIGRANT!

$73K

CBO LONG-TERM BUDGET OUTLOOK.

CBO LONG-TERM BUDGET OUTLOOK WITH DEFICIT REDUCTION.

ARE WE HEARING YOU RIGHT? SOUNDS LIKE YOU'RE SAYING IMMIGRATION WILL SAVE SOCIAL SECURITY AND MEDICARE.

IT'S COMPLICATED. ACCORDING TO OFFICIAL PROJECTIONS, A LARGER DOSE OF THE CURRENT IMMIGRANT MIX WOULD DO THE TRICK.

"THE CURRENT IMMIGRANT MIX"? STOP BEATING AROUND THE BUSH, SONNY—AND TELL US WHAT WE REALLY WANT TO KNOW!

YEAH! WE KEEP HEARING THAT FISCAL DISASTER IS ON THE HORIZON. WILL OPEN BORDERS PAINLESSLY SAVE THE DAY?

DON'T GET YOUR HOPES UP.

FOR THOSE WHO FINISH HIGH SCHOOL, BUT DON'T GO TO COLLEGE, NPV IS STILL POSITIVE: $49,000 PER IMMIGRANT.

BUT FOR THOSE WHO DIDN'T FINISH HIGH SCHOOL, THE OVERALL, LONG-RUN FISCAL EFFECT IS NEGATIVE: -$117,000 PER IMMIGRANT.

OVERALL LONG-RUN FISCAL EFFECTS REMAIN POSITIVE IF WE FOCUS ON *YOUNG* LOW-SKILL IMMIGRANTS.

IMMIGRATED WHEN LESS THAN TWENTY-FIVE YEARS OLD:

HIGH SCHOOL ONLY:
$239K

LESS THAN HIGH SCHOOL:
$35K

BUT OLDER LOW-SKILL IMMIGRANTS' FISCAL EFFECTS ARE CORRESPONDINGLY NEGATIVE.

IMMIGRATED WHEN SIXTY-FIVE-PLUS:

HIGH SCHOOL ONLY:
-$164K

LESS THAN HIGH SCHOOL:
-$257K

BOTTOM LINE: WHEN NOBEL PRIZE-WINNING ECONOMIST MILTON FRIEDMAN SAID...

"YOU CANNOT SIMULTANEOUSLY HAVE FREE IMMIGRATION AND A WELFARE STATE"...

HE WAS *WRONG.*

FREE IMMIGRATION WITH A U.S.-STYLE WELFARE STATE IS *NOT* A RECIPE FOR FISCAL DISASTER. EVEN UNDER OPEN BORDERS, THE BURDENSOME IMMIGRANT WOULD BE THE EXCEPTION, NOT THE RULE.

HARRUMPH! WHY LET IN ANY BURDENSOME IMMIGRANTS AT ALL?

MILTON! I'M SURPRISED AT YOU. THAT'S WHAT YOU SAY AFTER A LIFETIME PROMOTING HUMAN FREEDOM?

I'VE NEVER BEEN AN ABSOLUTIST.

NOR AM I. BUT WE'RE NOT TALKING ABOUT A MINOR ABRIDGMENT OF FREEDOM FOR VAST SOCIAL GAIN. QUITE THE OPPOSITE.

IF YOU PICTURE IMMIGRANTS AS CHARITY CASES...

OPEN BORDERS ADMITTEDLY SOUNDS LIKE SUICIDAL ALTRUISM.

WHY SHOULD *WE* HAVE TO CARRY THE WHOLE WORLD ON OUR SHOULDERS?

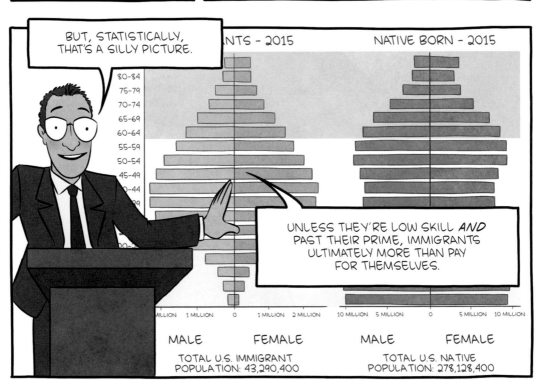

BUT, STATISTICALLY, THAT'S A SILLY PICTURE.

NTS - 2015

NATIVE BORN - 2015

80-84
75-79
70-74
65-69
60-64
55-59
50-54
45-49
-44

UNLESS THEY'RE LOW SKILL *AND* PAST THEIR PRIME, IMMIGRANTS ULTIMATELY MORE THAN PAY FOR THEMSELVES.

MILLION 1 MILLION 0 1 MILLION 2 MILLION

10 MILLION 5 MILLION 0 5 MILLION 10 MILLION

MALE   FEMALE

MALE   FEMALE

TOTAL U.S. IMMIGRANT POPULATION: 43,290,400

TOTAL U.S. NATIVE POPULATION: 278,128,400

WHY THEN ARE APPEALS TO THE "NATIVE'S BURDEN" SO COMPELLING? BECAUSE IMMIGRANTS ARE IDEAL **SCAPEGOATS** FOR NATIONS' FISCAL IRRESPONSIBILITY.

WHY DO MATH WHEN YOU CAN HASTILY POINT FINGERS AT FOREIGNERS?

IF FISCAL CRISIS EVER **DOES** HIT, LOTS OF PEOPLE WILL BLAME "OPEN BORDERS," EVEN THOUGH OUR BORDERS ARE ANYTHING BUT OPEN.

HOW IS THIS **MY** FAULT?!

OPEN BORDERS IS ADMITTEDLY NO QUICK FIX FOR AMERICA'S FISCAL WOES.

BUT OUTCRY OVER THE NATIVE'S BURDEN IS SADLY INNUMERATE. IF YOU'RE LOOKING FOR AN INTELLECTUALLY RESPECTABLE REASON TO **REJECT** OPEN BORDERS...

YOU'D BETTER FIND ANOTHER PROBLEM TO PIN ON ME.

CHAPTER 4

CRIMES AGAINST CULTURE

AS A FANBOY OF WESTERN CULTURE, I TAKE THESE CONCERNS SERIOUSLY.

FOR ALL OUR SHORTCOMINGS AND HYPOCRISIES, THE ENLIGHTENMENT IDEALS OF THE WEST UNDERLIE THE PROSPERITY, PEACE, FREEDOM, AND JUSTICE THAT THE FIRST WORLD TAKES FOR GRANTED.

CONSIDER HOW MUCH WE OWE TO VALUES LIKE...

Socrates

TOLERANCE

Voltaire

"THE JEW, THE MAHOMETAN, AND THE CHRISTIAN TRANSACT TOGETHER, AS THOUGH THEY ALL PROFESSED THE SAME RELIGION, AND GIVE THE NAME OF INFIDEL TO NONE BUT BANKRUPTS."

UNIVERSAL HUMAN RIGHTS

Tubman

AM I NOT A WOMAN AND A SISTER?

BUT WHEN I APPEAL TO THESE VALUES TO MAKE THE CASE FOR OPEN BORDERS, FELLOW FANS OF WESTERN CULTURE OFTEN PUSH BACK.

LET'S START WITH THE MOST EMOTIONALLY POWERFUL ANTI-IMMIGRATION ARGUMENT IN THE UNIVERSE...

TERRORISM!

INDISCRIMINATELY MURDERING THE INNOCENT IS UNTHINKABLY EVIL.

Generic Action Hero

DAMMIT! I'M TOO LATE!

AND IN THE FIRST WORLD, THE FOREIGN-BORN ARE RESPONSIBLE FOR MOST TERRORISM. FROM 1975 TO 2015, FOREIGN-BORN TERRORISTS WERE RESPONSIBLE FOR 88% OF ALL TERRORISM DEATHS ON U.S. SOIL.

DAMMIT! THEY'VE GOT TO BE STOPPED!

AND THAT'S WHY THE SEEMINGLY HARDHEADED "SKITTLES ARGUMENT" AGAINST IMMIGRATION IS THE HEIGHT OF INNUMERACY.

If I had a bowl of *Skittles* and I told you just three would kill you, Would you take a handful?

That's our **Syrian refugee problem.**

IF THERE ARE THREE POISON PILLS IN A BOWL WITH MANY *MILLIONS* OF CANDIES, REFUSING TO EAT IS AS CHILDISH AS...

REFUSING TO GET IN A CAR BECAUSE YOU "MIGHT" GET IN AN ACCIDENT...

OR REFUSING TO LEAVE YOUR HOUSE BECAUSE YOU "MIGHT" BE STRUCK BY LIGHTNING.

THE INNUMERATE LIFE...

IS NOT WORTH LIVING!

AAAA!

STORIES WITH FEARLESS HEROES WHO STAND BETWEEN US AND TERRORIST ANNIHILATION MAKE GRIPPING FICTION.

DAMMIT! THE WORLD ALMOST ENDS EVERY SINGLE DAY!

BUT THESE STORIES ARE JUST MORBID FANTASIES. TREATING THE MICROSCOPIC RISK OF TERRORISM AS "PROOF" OF OUR "CULTURAL SICKNESS" IS CRAZY.

DAMMIT! I'M NOT A NUMBERS GUY!

AND USING THESE ULTRA-RARE TRAGEDIES TO EXCLUDE THE 99.9999% OF IMMIGRANTS WHO AREN'T TERRORISTS IS A CRIME.

CRIMINOLOGISTS ALSO MEASURE IMMIGRATION'S BROADER EFFECT ON CRIME RATES.

Welcome to MIAMI BEACH

DO IMMIGRANTS SOMEHOW DISRUPT THE SOCIAL ORDER, DRIVING *NATIVES* TO CRIME?

SAY HELLO TO MY LITTLE FRIEND!

IN 2016, THE NATIONAL ACADEMY OF SCIENCES SCRUTINIZED DECADES OF RESEARCH, CONCLUDING "THE PRESENCE OF LARGE NUMBERS OF IMMIGRANTS SEEMS TO *LOWER* CRIME RATES."

The Integration of Immigrants into American Society

THE ONLY BAD NEWS IS THAT IMMIGRANTS' VIRTUE ISN'T HEREDITARY. LATER GENERATIONS ULTIMATELY "ASSIMILATE" TO HIGHER *AMERICAN* CRIME RATES.

I NEVER WANTED THIS LIFE FOR YOU, MICHAEL.

IT'S THE AMERICAN WAY, POPS!

NUMERACY WON'T MEND YOUR HEART IF AN IMMIGRANT KILLS SOMEONE YOU LOVE.

BUT NUMERACY WILL PREVENT YOU FROM USING ONE INJUSTICE TO RATIONALIZE ANOTHER.

IF A REDHEAD MURDERS, WE DON'T LASH OUT AT REDHEADS IN GENERAL.

"Aurora Killer" James Holmes

WE PUNISH THE GUILTY REDHEAD.

THERE'S NO REASON TO TREAT IMMIGRANTS WORSE THAN REDHEADS.

IF AN IMMIGRANT MURDERS, WE SHOULDN'T DEPRIVE IMMIGRANTS IN GENERAL OF THE FREEDOM TO LIVE AND WORK WHERE THEY PLEASE.

...WITH LIBERTY, JUSTICE, AND NUMERACY FOR ALL.

WE SHOULD PUNISH THE GUILTY IMMIGRANT.

A CENTURY LATER, LITTLE HAS CHANGED. A LARGE MAJORITY OF *FIRST*-GENERATION KIDS SPEAK ENGLISH WELL. RATES FOR LATER GENERATIONS APPROACH 100%. THIS IS TRUE EVEN FOR GROUPS THAT ALLEGEDLY "DON'T LEARN ENGLISH," LIKE...

ENGLISH SKILLS—ASIAN KIDS (AGES 6–15), BY GENERATION

ENGLISH SKILLS—HISPANIC KIDS (AGES 6–15), BY GENERATION

NOTE: SINCE WE'RE TALKING ABOUT KIDS, THESE NUMBERS *UNDER*STATE ENGLISH FLUENCY. MY WIFE, WHO IMMIGRATED WHEN SHE WAS SEVEN, NOW SPEAKS ROMANIAN WITH AN AMERICAN ACCENT, NOT ENGLISH WITH A ROMANIAN ACCENT.

IF YOU WANT THE **REAL** STORY OF
ASSIMILATION, ASK AN IMMIGRANT PARENT...

MY SON JAYESH SPEAKS HINDI PERFECTLY—AND ALL MY GRANDKIDS ARE FLUENT, TOO!

THEY COULDN'T CARE LESS ABOUT AMERICAN CULTURE. IT'S ALL *INDIA, INDIA, INDIA* FOR THEM!

WHAT IMMIGRANT PARENTS *NEVER SAY*

MY SON JAYESH WON'T EVEN SPEAK OUR LANGUAGE. WHATEVER I SAY, HE RESPONDS IN ENGLISH. MY GRANDKIDS DON'T KNOW A *WORD* OF HINDI!

OUR CULTURE MEANS NOTHING TO THEM. BOLLYWOOD, CRICKET, GANDHI—IT'S ALL THE SAME AS FAR AS THEY'RE CONCERNED!

WHAT THEY *ALWAYS SAY*

RESEARCHERS ACTUALLY MEASURE "LINGUISTIC LIFE EXPECTANCIES"— THE AVERAGE NUMBER OF GENERATIONS A FOREIGN LANGUAGE SURVIVES. HERE ARE THE NUMBERS FOR "MULTICULTURAL" SOUTHERN CALIFORNIA:

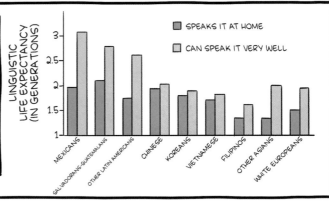

LINGUISTIC LIFE EXPECTANCY (IN GENERATIONS)

- SPEAKS IT AT HOME
- CAN SPEAK IT VERY WELL

MEXICANS · SALVADORANS-GUATEMALANS · OTHER LATIN AMERICANS · CHINESE · KOREANS · VIETNAMESE · FILIPINOS · OTHER ASIANS · WHITE EUROPEANS

ON AVERAGE, FOR EXAMPLE, IT TAKES LESS THAN TWO GENERATIONS FOR KOREAN IMMIGRANTS TO LOSE KOREAN FLUENCY.

1.75
1
KOREANS

WHAT'S SPECIAL ABOUT HISPANICS IN PLACES LIKE CALIFORNIA ISN'T THAT THEY "DON'T LEARN ENGLISH," BUT THAT THEY RETAIN FLUENT SPANISH FOR ONE EXTRA GENERATION!

MEXICANS · SALVADORANS-GUATEMALANS · OTHER LATIN AMERICANS

MODERN COMMUNICATION AND TRANSPORTATION DEFINITELY MAKE IT EASIER FOR IMMIGRANTS TO *NOT* ASSIMILATE THAN A CENTURY AGO.

BUT THAT'S ONLY HALF THE STORY.

MODERN COMMUNICATION AND TRANSPORTATION ALSO MAKE IT EASIER FOR FOREIGNERS TO *PRE*-ASSIMILATE: TO AMERICANIZE BEFORE THEY IMMIGRATE!

MEASURED BY *NATIVE* SPEAKERS, ENGLISH IS ONLY THE THIRD MOST-SPOKEN LANGUAGE ON EARTH, AFTER MANDARIN AND SPANISH.

BUT MEASURED BY *ALL* SPEAKERS, ENGLISH IS THE *MOST*-SPOKEN LANGUAGE ON EARTH!

PRE-ASSIMILATION!

BUT WHAT ABOUT ASSIMILATION?

IT WON'T SAVE YOU. TRUST IS SHOCKINGLY STABLE.

SWEDEN'S WAY MORE TRUSTING THAN THE U.S., BUT SWEDISH AMERICANS ARE ABOUT AS TRUSTING AS HOME-GROWN SWEDES!

STOCKHOLM

MINNEAPOLIS

ARE YOU SERIOUSLY GOING TO *TRUST* THIS GUY? LET'S LOOK AT THE DATA.

WHILE TRUST IS FAIRLY PERSISTENT, FOLKS WHO LEAVE LOW-TRUST COUNTRIES HAVE MARKEDLY HIGHER TRUST THAN FOLKS WHO STAY BEHIND.

Refugees Welcome!

CHANGING THE PEOPLE YOU SEE CHANGES THE WAY YOU SEE PEOPLE.

FOR DESCENDANTS OF WILLING IMMIGRANTS, TRUST ASSIMILATION IS ALMOST COMPLETE.

"MOST PEOPLE CAN BE TRUSTED"

% U.S. NATIVES WHO SAY YES

100
80
60
40
20

HOW PERFECT TRUST *PERSISTENCE* WOULD WORK

HOW TRUST *ASSIMILATION* ACTUALLY WORKS

20 40 60 80 100
% IN ANCESTRAL COUNTRY WHO SAY YES

HERE'S WHAT HAPPENS IF WE USE AVERAGE TRUST IN YOUR ANCESTRAL COUNTRY TO PREDICT YOUR TRUST IN THE U.S.

SWEDISH AMERICANS *ARE* UNUSUALLY TRUSTING. BUT AS A RULE, TRUST IS A LOT MORE LIKE LANGUAGE THAN HAIR COLOR.

IN ANY CASE, TRUST IS OVERRATED.

Dude...

WHAT IS IT WITH ECONOMISTS?

SURE, YOU NEED *MODERATE* TRUST FOR A FUNCTIONAL SOCIETY.

BUT THE HIGHEST-TRUST PARTS OF AMERICA ARE PLACES LIKE THE DAKOTAS, NEW HAMPSHIRE, AND MONTANA—AND THE LOWEST-TRUST ARE PLACES LIKE SAN FRANCISCO, BOSTON, HOUSTON, AND DENVER. DO THESE CITIES REALLY SCARE YOU?

SEE YOU IN HELL, L.A.!

Trust Bust

COULD BE A STATISTICAL FLUKE, BUT MODERATE TRUST SEEMS BETTER FOR NATIONAL PROSPERITY THAN *EITHER* EXTREME.

PARTIAL REGRESSION PLOT FOR 23 OECD COUNTRIES— TRUST AND ECONOMIC GROWTH (1980-2004)

Not trusting enough.

Too trusting?

ANNUAL GDP GROWTH

5%
4%
3%
2%
1%
0%

0   20   40   60   80

% WHO TRUST

THE SAME GOES FOR PERSONAL PROSPERITY. THE ULTRA-TRUSTING EARN LESS THAN THE PRUDENTLY TRUSTING. THEY EVEN GET CHEATED MORE!

WE'D ALWAYS LIKE PEOPLE TO BE MORE TRUST*WORTHY,* BUT WE HAVE PLENTY OF SYNONYMS FOR "OVERLY TRUSTING."

OBLIVIOUS!

CLUELESS!

CARELESS!

NAIVE!

MY RULE OF THUMB:

WE NEED ENOUGH TRUST TO MAKE CREDIT CARDS WORK.

COSMOPOLITANISM MAY NOT SOUND LIKE THE BASIS FOR CULTURAL GREATNESS.

BUT ITS OPEN, COMPETITIVE SPIRIT GIVES ALL OF US THE OPPORTUNITY TO PICK AND CHOOSE THE BEST ELEMENTS OF EVERY CULTURE ON EARTH!

THE BEST LIFESTYLES!

THE BEST ART!

THE BEST FOOD!

WE SHOULD EXPECT THE ENEMIES OF WESTERN
CULTURE TO PREDICT ITS DEMISE.

Khomeini

THE ATHEIST
WEST IS
DOOMED!

Trotsky

THE CAPITALIST
WEST IS
DOOMED!

Mugabe

THE RACIST
WEST IS
DOOMED!

WHAT'S WEIRD IS THAT
SO MANY *FRIENDS* OF
WESTERN CULTURE
SAY THE SAME.

AS REPRESSIVE REGIMES AROUND
THE WORLD FIGHT A LOSING BATTLE
TO KEEP WESTERN CULTURE OUT.

THE
AWESOME
WEST IS
DOOMED!

MANY IN THE WEST
SEE NON-WESTERN
IMMIGRANTS AND SAY:

THEY'LL
NEVER
FIT IN!

BUT FRIEND OR FOE OF WESTERN CULTURE, THE DOOMSAYERS ARE WRONG.

FIRST-GENERATION IMMIGRANTS HAVE NEVER FULLY ASSIMILATED. BUT THEIR KIDS DON'T JUST EMBRACE WESTERN CULTURE. THEY REVITALIZE IT.

CULTURAL PESSIMISTS NEED TO FORGET SHOCKING HEADLINES AND PLEDGE THEMSELVES TO NUMERACY. WESTERNIZATION ISN'T A NAIVE DREAM. IT'S ALL AROUND US.

OR, AS A GREAT EASTERN PHILOSOPHER SUPPOSEDLY* SAID:

Confucius

THE MAN WHO SAYS IT CANNOT BE DONE SHOULD NOT INTERRUPT THOSE WHO ARE DOING IT.

*NOT REALLY, BUT HE SHOULD HAVE.

CHAPTER 5
THE GOLDEN GOOSE ON TRIAL

BY HISTORICAL AND WORLD STANDARDS, CITIZENS
OF THE FIRST WORLD ENJOY MANY FREEDOMS.

SURE, THIS **SOUNDS** LIKE A DEMENTEDLY STUPID PLAN.

Master Plan
1. Flee hellhole of birth.
2. Get first-world citizenship.
3. Vote Hellhole Party.
4. Repeat.

IF YOU HATE FREEDOM, WHY NOT HATE IT FROM AFAR?

BUT IMMIGRATION CRITICS CAN PLAUSIBLY REPLY: "MOST PEOPLE WHO HATE FREEDOM STILL LOVE PROSPERITY. FREEDOM-HATERS COME FOR GOOD JOBS, HOPING TO END FREEDOM ONCE THEY HAVE THE VOTES."

DOESN'T OUR FREEDOM **CAUSE** OUR PROSPERITY? ONLY IN THE LONG RUN, SO IT'S EASY FOR FREEDOM-HATERS TO SCOFF AND DENY.

IF YOU THINK EVERYONE VOTES IN THEIR ENLIGHTENED SELF-INTEREST, YOU CAN SUMMARILY DISMISS THIS STORY.

BUT THAT'S PRETTY CRAZY!

VOTERS ARE HIGHLY IRRATIONAL.

SOME ECON PROFESSOR EVEN WROTE A BOOK ON IT.

my first book!

IF YOU'RE WORRIED ABOUT THE POLITICAL DANGER OF IMMIGRATION, OF COURSE, THE KEY QUESTION ISN'T "ARE IMMIGRANTS BAD VOTERS?" BUT "ARE IMMIGRANTS *WORSE* VOTERS THAN NATIVES?"

WHICH RAISES THE UNAVOIDABLE QUESTION: "WORSE BY WHAT STANDARD?"

FOR PARTISANS, THE ANSWER IS OBVIOUS: IMMIGRANTS WHO VOTE *FOR* MY PARTY ARE GOOD. IMMIGRANTS WHO VOTE *AGAINST* MY PARTY ARE BAD.

BACK IN THE 1980S, NATIVE AND IMMIGRANT VOTING WAS ALMOST IDENTICAL. BUT OVER THE LAST TWENTY-FIVE YEARS, A BIG GAP HAS OPENED UP: DEMOCRATIC PRESIDENTIAL CANDIDATES NOW DO ABOUT TEN PERCENTAGE POINTS BETTER WITH IMMIGRANTS THAN WITH NATIVES.

DEMOCRATS ARE EVEN MORE POPULAR WITH IMMIGRANTS WHO *DON'T* OR *CAN'T* VOTE. BETWEEN 2004 AND 2012, THE DEMOCRATS' EDGE LEAPT FROM ELEVEN TO TWENTY-EIGHT POINTS!

THIS ISN'T JUST ABOUT RACE. BY 2012, *WHITE* IMMIGRANTS VOTED NINE PERCENTAGE POINTS MORE DEMOCRATIC THAN WHITE NATIVES.

REPUBLICANS HAVE A HANDY EXPLANATION: SELF-INTEREST. PEOPLE VOTE FOR PARTIES THAT DELIVER POLICIES THAT BENEFIT THEM.

BUT REPUBLICANS DO POORLY EVEN WITH WEALTHY, SOCIALLY CONSERVATIVE ASIAN IMMIGRANTS. THINK ABOUT INDIAN AMERICANS.

WE'RE AMERICA'S RICHEST ETHNICITY.

ALMOST ALL OUR KIDS HAVE TWO MARRIED PARENTS.

AND OUR DEMOCRATIC/ REPUBLICAN RATIO IS 4:1!

IMMIGRANTS WANT HANDOUTS, PAID FOR BY HARD-WORKING NATIVES!

IN ANY CASE, UNLESS YOU'RE A PROFESSIONAL POLITICIAN, WHAT COUNTS ISN'T WHICH PARTY WINS, BUT WHAT POLICIES THEY ADOPT. AND *THAT* DEPENDS CRUCIALLY ON VOTERS' POLICY VIEWS.

THE CRUCIAL QUESTION, THEN, IS WHAT DO IMMIGRANTS THINK ABOUT *POLICY*?

LOOK AT HOW TEXAS DEMOCRATS AND MASSACHUSETTS REPUBLICANS "GO NATIVE" TO WIN VOTES!

115

ALEX NOWRASTEH OF THE CATO INSTITUTE KNOWS THE NUMBERS. WHAT THE AVERAGE IMMIGRANT THINKS ABOUT POLICY IS...

PRETTY MUCH WHAT THE AVERAGE NATIVE THINKS.

POLITICAL IDEOLOGY (2000-2016)

AVERAGE IMMIGRANT (3.98)

AVERAGE NATIVE (4.16)

1 VERY LIBERAL   2   3   4 MODERATE   5   6   7 VERY CONSERVATIVE

THE AVERAGE IMMIGRANT IS MICROSCOPICALLY MORE LIBERAL THAN THE AVERAGE NATIVE.

"SHOULD GOVERNMENT DO MORE OR LESS?" (2000-2016)

AVERAGE NATIVE (2.89)

AVERAGE IMMIGRANT (3.33)

"GOVERNMENT IN WASHINGTON IS TRYING TO DO TOO MANY THINGS THAT SHOULD BE LEFT TO INDIVIDUALS AND PRIVATE BUSINESS."

"GOVERNMENT SHOULD DO EVEN MORE TO SOLVE OUR COUNTRY'S PROBLEMS."

1   2   3   4   5

THE AVERAGE IMMIGRANT IS *MODESTLY* MORE IN FAVOR OF GOVERNMENT ACTIVISM.

"TAXES ON *X* ARE..." (2000-2016)

"THE RICH" NATIVE: 2.79 IMMIGRANT: 3.06

"THE MIDDLE CLASS" NATIVE: 3.60 IMMIGRANT: 3.55

"THE POOR" NATIVE: 3.74 IMMIGRANT: 3.69

1 MUCH TOO LOW   2   3 ABOUT RIGHT   4   5 MUCH TOO HIGH

THE AVERAGE IMMIGRANT IS ALMOST EXACTLY AS HOSTILE AS NATIVES TO TAXES ON THE POOR AND MIDDLE CLASS—AND SLIGHTLY *MORE* HOSTILE THAN NATIVES TO TAXES ON THE RICH.

IF YOU LOOK CLOSER, IMMIGRANTS SUPPORT WELFARE *SLIGHTLY* MORE THAN NATIVES.

BUT IMMIGRANTS ARE ALSO SLIGHTLY *LESS* SUPPORTIVE OF GOVERNMENT SPENDING ON SOCIAL SECURITY, HEALTH, EDUCATION, AND THE ENVIRONMENT—AND NOTICEABLY LESS SUPPORTIVE OF DEFENSE SPENDING.

IT'S ALL RELATIVE, OF COURSE. MOST OF THESE PROGRAMS ARE *EXTREMELY* POPULAR WITH NATIVE AND IMMIGRANT ALIKE.

ON SOCIAL ISSUES, IMMIGRANTS ARE RELIABLY, BUT MODESTLY, MORE CONSERVATIVE THAN NATIVES...

ABORTION ON DEMAND?

GAY MARRIAGE?

LEGALIZE MARIJUANA?

FREE SPEECH FOR RADICAL MUSLIMS?

WITH ONE PREDICTABLE EXCEPTION.

LET IN MORE IMMIGRANTS?

EVEN THIS GAP IS NOTHING RADICAL: ONLY 27% OF IMMIGRANTS FAVOR *MORE* IMMIGRATION—VERSUS 12% OF NATIVES.

BUT I HAVE TO TELL YOU: THERE IS ONE BIG SUBSET OF IMMIGRANTS THAT DIVERGES MORE FROM MAINSTREAM AMERICAN OPINION.

A SUBSET WHOSE LOW SUPPORT FOR PERSONAL AND ECONOMIC FREEDOM STANDS OUT.

CURRENT IMMIGRATION LAW STERNLY DISCRIMINATES AGAINST THEM, SO THEY'D BE FAR MORE COMMON IF MY CASE FOR OPEN BORDERS ACTUALLY CAUGHT ON.

I'M TALKING ABOUT...

LOW-SKILLED IMMIGRANTS.

EVEN OTHERWISE TOLERANT PEOPLE OFTEN BADMOUTH AND DEHUMANIZE LOW-SKILLED IMMIGRANTS. THROUGHOUT THIS BOOK I'VE TRIED TO DO THE OPPOSITE—TO HIGHLIGHT NOT ONLY THEIR NEGLECTED CONTRIBUTIONS, BUT THEIR BASIC HUMAN RIGHTS.

BUT I'VE WORKED WITH THE DATA, AND I'M HONESTLY TROUBLED BY LOW-SKILLED FOREIGNERS' VIEWS ON ISSUES LIKE FREE SPEECH...

SUPPORT FOR FREE SPEECH

IMMIGRANTS WITHOUT HIGH SCHOOL DEGREES

OTHER IMMIGRANTS

U.S. MEAN

1 10 20 30 40 50 60 70 80 90 99
PERCENTILE

AND GOVERNMENT'S ROLE IN THE ECONOMY.

IMMIGRANTS WITHOUT HIGH SCHOOL DEGREES

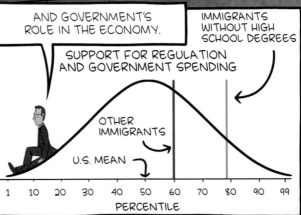

SUPPORT FOR REGULATION AND GOVERNMENT SPENDING

OTHER IMMIGRANTS

U.S. MEAN

1 10 20 30 40 50 60 70 80 90 99
PERCENTILE

OF COURSE, IF YOU THINK THE U.S. IS ALREADY TOO ECONOMICALLY CONSERVATIVE OR TOO SOCIALLY LIBERAL, I'VE GIVEN YOU CAUSE FOR *DISAPPOINTMENT* RATHER THAN RELIEF.

IMMIGRATION'S UNLIKELY TO NOTICEABLY TILT THE POLITICAL SCALES IN YOUR FAVOR.

BUT THAT'S HARDLY A REASON TO *OPPOSE* IMMIGRATION.

SOME LEFT-LEANING SCHOLARS, HOWEVER, ARGUE THAT IMMIGRATION SOURS *NATIVES* ON THE WELFARE STATE.

HOW? BY UNDERMINING NATIONAL SOLIDARITY.

PEOPLE DON'T LIKE PAYING TAXES TO SUPPORT OUT-GROUPS.

ONE EXPERIMENT IN NORWAY FOUND THAT PUBLIC SUPPORT FOR A MINIMUM INCOME PROGRAM FALLS FROM 66% TO 45% IF YOU *MENTION* THAT NON-CITIZENS WOULD BE ELIGIBLE.

BUT THIS IS SOMEWHAT SPECULATIVE. IF YOU LOOK AT BUDGETS OF FIRST-WORLD COUNTRIES WITH RELATIVELY HIGH IMMIGRATION, THE WELFARE STATE IS STILL GOING STRONG.

IN ANY CASE, IF YOU WANT TO HELP THE NEEDY, EXCLUDING DESTITUTE FOREIGNERS TO PROTECT YOUR DOMESTIC WELFARE STATE SEEMS PRETTY PERVERSE.

MY FUNDAMENTAL REPLY TO THESE CRITICS: I DON'T BELIEVE IN "MAGIC DIRT." WHAT I BELIEVE IN IS...

MAGIC CULTURE!

WHEN FIRST-WORLD COUNTRIES WELCOME THE "TIRED AND POOR" FROM EVEN THE MOST BACKWARD AND AUTHORITARIAN NATIONS, THESE IMMIGRANTS QUICKLY ACCULTURATE *ENOUGH* TO BECOME PRODUCTIVE MEMBERS OF OUR SOCIETY.

AND WHATEVER "OLD COUNTRY WAYS" THEIR PARENTS TEACH THEM, THE CHILDREN OF IMMIGRANTS WHO GROW UP HERE DEEPLY ACCULTURATE TO THEIR NEW HOME.

CULTURE TAKES CENTURIES TO SPREAD BY PERSUASION, BUT ONLY ONE GENERATION TO SPREAD BY...

IMMERSION!

AT LEAST THAT'S HOW IT SEEMS TO ME. COULD I BE WRONG?

IN RECENT YEARS, SOME TOP RESEARCHERS HAVE ARGUED THAT *ANCESTRY* IS A POWERFUL FORCE.

TODAY'S MOST DEVELOPED NATIONS ARE LARGELY POPULATED BY FOLKS WHOSE ANCESTORS WERE *RELATIVELY* ADVANCED BY 1500 A.D.

THIS IS TRUE EVEN IN THE AMERICAS...

AND OCEANIA!

THE HISTORY IS HORRIFYING—CENTURIES OF CONQUEST, SLAVERY, AND EVEN GENOCIDE—BUT THE PATTERNS PRACTICALLY JUMP OFF THE MAP.

THE SOURCE OF THIS PERSISTENCE COULD BE *ENTIRELY* CULTURAL. THE RESEARCHERS' KEY CLAIM IS SIMPLY THAT IF THEY KNOW HOW ADVANCED YOUR NATION'S ANCESTORS WERE CENTURIES AGO, THEY CAN MAKE PRETTY GOOD PREDICTIONS ABOUT YOUR NATION TODAY.

PRACTICALLY SPEAKING, THOUGH, SAYING "IT'S ALL CULTURAL" IS SMALL COMFORT.

IF ADVANCED CIVILIZATIONS' SURVIVAL HINGES ON CULTURAL ANCESTRY, OPEN BORDERS STILL SOUNDS LIKE A PATH TO FIRST-WORLD SUICIDE.

IT'S TEMPTING TO QUESTION ANCESTRY RESEARCHERS' MOTIVES, BUT LET'S FACE THEIR WORK HEAD-ON.

DAMMIT! DO YOUR WORST!

OKAY. THE BIGGEST FLAW WITH THIS RESEARCH IS...

THAT IT GROSSLY *UNDER*-PREDICTS DEVELOPMENT FOR THE UNITED STATES, WHICH LEADS THE WORLD DESPITE MEDIOCRE ANCESTRY SCORES...

Silicon Valley

Deep-Fried Cheese Curds

L.A.

Texas Triangle

Chicago

NYC

AND GROSSLY *OVER*PREDICTS DEVELOPMENT FOR CHINA AND INDIA, WHICH LAG DESPITE EXCELLENT ANCESTRY SCORES.

Extremely poor interior provinces

Beijing

Chengdu

Hangzhou

Shenzhen

Shanghai

New Delhi

Hong Kong

Mumbai

Wealthier developing cities

1,200
1,100
1,000
900
800
700
600
500
400
300
200
100

JAPAN

CHINA   INDIA   USA   BRAZIL   NIGERIA   RUSSIA
INDONESIA   PAKISTAN   BANGLADESH

10 MOST POPULOUS COUNTRIES
(IN MILLIONS)

YOU COULD MINIMIZE THESE AS MERE "OUTLIERS," BUT WE'RE TALKING ABOUT EARTH'S THREE MOST POPULOUS COUNTRIES, CONTAINING OVER 40% OF THE HUMAN RACE.

STATISTICALLY, THE PROBLEM IS THAT RESEARCHERS PUT EQUAL WEIGHT ON ALL COUNTRIES.

IF YOU WEIGH COUNTRIES BY POPULATION AND RECRUNCH THE NUMBERS, ANCESTRY LOOKS UNIMPORTANT.

DAMMIT! THE RESULTS ARE FRAGILE!

DAMMIT! WHY NOT?

TRUE. BUT EVEN IF THEY WERE ROCK SOLID, THE ANTI-IMMIGRATION SPIN IS NOT.

BECAUSE THE ORIGINAL RESEARCH ALSO FINDS HUGE EFFECTS OF *GEOGRAPHY*.

HOLDING ANCESTRY *FIXED*, COUNTRIES DO MUCH WORSE IF THEY'RE TROPICAL...

OR LANDLOCKED.

MONGOLIAN SHIPPING CO.

AS A RESULT, THIS WORK IMPLIES *MASSIVE* SOCIAL GAINS OF MIGRATION AWAY FROM THE TROPICS AND TOWARD THE COASTS.

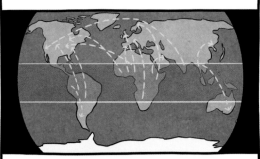

RATHER THAN UNDERMINING "OPEN BORDERS WOULD *DOUBLE* GLOBAL GDP" ESTIMATES, ANCESTRY RESEARCH CONFIRMS THEM!

WHILE ANCESTRY MODELS *DO* SAY MIGRATION FROM THE THIRD WORLD WILL LOWER AVERAGE GDP IN THE FIRST WORLD, THE MECHANISM IS GOOD ARITHMETIC, NOT BAD POLITICS.

OPEN BORDERS: [X]
ARITH. FALLACY: [0]

WELCOMING LOW-SKILLED IMMIGRANTS TO YOUR COUNTRY LOWERS AVERAGE GDP FOR THE SAME REASON WELCOMING CHILDREN TO YOUR BASKETBALL COURT LOWERS AVERAGE HEIGHT!

LAST, LET'S CALMLY CONSIDER THE **MOST** CONTROVERSIAL REASON TO FEAR THE LONG-RUN POLITICAL EFFECTS OF OPEN BORDERS.

HAVE YOU PONDERED A LITTLE THING CALLED... IQ?

IQ, PSYCHOLOGISTS' STANDARD MEASURE OF INTELLIGENCE, IS A GOOD PREDICTOR OF STANDARD FORMS OF SUCCESS.

ACADEMIC SUCCESS!

IQ Score: 130

120

135

CAREER SUCCESS!

135

2⁸

145

MARITAL SUCCESS!

HAPPY 30th ANNIVERSARY

IQ Scores
Hers: 115
His: 114

MANY WANT TO DISMISS IQ OUT OF HAND, BUT THAT'S HIGHLY IMPRUDENT.

IF RESEARCHERS FOUND THAT LEAD EXPOSURE HURT IQ, WOULD YOU REALLY OBJECT, "IQ IS MEANINGLESS"?

WITHOUT IQ TESTS, HOW WOULD WE EVEN MEASURE THE DANGER?

PLENTY. BOLD RESEARCHERS HAVE DISSECTED THE EFFECT OF NATIONAL IQ ON NATIONAL SUCCESS... MOST NOTABLY ECONOMIST GARETT JONES IN *HIVE MIND*.

MANY BRILLIANT INTELLECTS FIND HIS CASE DEEPLY COMPELLING.

THAT'S NOT NEWS TO ME.

GARETT HAS AN OFFICE JUST DOWN THE HALL FROM ME!

THE VIEW THAT NATIONAL IQ GENUINELY CAUSES NATIONAL SUCCESS MAKES GREAT SENSE. SMART PEOPLE AREN'T JUST MORE SKILLED. EXPERIMENTS ALSO SHOW THEY'RE BETTER COOPERATORS.

NATIONAL IQ PREDICTS NATIONAL PROSPERITY FAR BETTER THAN EDUCATION, DEMOCRACY, OR VIRTUALLY ANYTHING ELSE.

THIS IS NO SIMPLEMINDED "ARITHMETIC FALLACY." THE EFFECT OF NATIONAL IQ ON NATIONAL PROSPERITY *FAR* EXCEEDS THE EFFECT OF INDIVIDUAL IQ ON INDIVIDUAL PROSPERITY, SUGGESTING MAJOR IQ "SPILLOVERS."

YOU'RE BETTER OFF HAVING A LOW IQ IN A HIGH-IQ SOCIETY THAN A HIGH IQ IN A LOW-IQ SOCIETY!

SINCE YOU FEAR LOW-IQ VOTERS, CONSIDER AN EXTREME CASE: THE WHOLE WORLD MOVES HERE, DRAGGING U.S. IQ DOWN TO THE *CURRENT* WORLD AVERAGE:

CURRENT U.S. IQ:
98
CURRENT WORLD IQ:
87

AN ELEVEN-POINT FALL. *DOOM!*

LET'S DO THE MATH. ACCORDING TO *HIVE MIND'S* MAIN ESTIMATE, U.S. PER-CAPITA GDP WOULD FALL FROM ITS CURRENT LEVEL OF $57,600 TO...?

OPEN BORDERS GDP
= 0.51 * CURRENT GDP
≈ $29,400

$29,400! A 49% DROP!

GROSS *WORLD* PRODUCT PER CAPITA IS NOW ROUGHLY $16,200. WHAT HAPPENS TO THAT?

$$\frac{\text{NEW GDP}}{\text{OLD GDP}} = \frac{\$29,400}{\$16,200} \approx +81\%$$

IT... ROUGHLY DOUBLES.

WHAT?! DO YOU MEAN TO TELL ME THAT DESPITE YOUR DOOMSAYING, YOU REACH ALMOST EXACTLY THE SAME RADICALLY PRO-IMMIGRATION NUMBERS AS MICHAEL CLEMENS?!

OPEN BORDERS **DOUBLES** GLOBAL PRODUCTION!

(BEST GUESS.)

IT'S ONLY THE BASIC MODEL. *HIVE MIND* INVESTIGATES AN ARRAY OF SUBTLETIES!

YOU'RE ABSOLUTELY RIGHT, BUT THE SUBTLETIES MAKE IMMIGRATION LOOK FAR *BETTER!*

SO FAR, ESTIMATES ASSUME CAUSATION GOES IN ONLY ONE DIRECTION: IQ RAISES WEALTH. BUT *HIVE MIND* DOCUMENTS MANY FORMS OF *REVERSE* CAUSATION, WHERE WEALTH RAISES IQ!

CREDIBLE CANDIDATES INCLUDE...

BETTER NUTRITION!

Iodized Salt

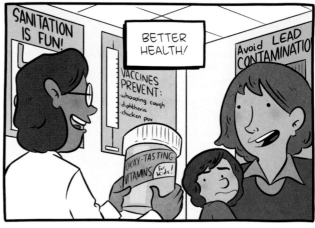

BETTER HEALTH!

SANITATION IS FUN!

Avoid LEAD CONTAMINATIO

VACCINES PREVENT:
·whooping cough
·diphtheria
·chicken pox

OKAY-TASTING VITAMINS *for kids!*

BETTER EDUCATION!

Anselm

Large Lizard

Cookie Abomination

Numeracy Werewolf

Sad Trash Gremlin

321 SUNFLOWER STREET

THE BEST WAY TO MEASURE THE COMBINED EFFECT OF ALL THESE FACTORS IS TO SEE WHAT HAPPENS WHEN PEOPLE FROM FIRST-WORLD COUNTRIES...

...*ADOPT* KIDS FROM THIRD-WORLD COUNTRIES!

THE BEST DATA COMES FROM SWEDEN, FAMOUS FOR ITS METICULOUS RECORD-KEEPING.

THE BABIES SWEDES ADOPT FROM PLACES LIKE INDIA, THAILAND, CHILE, SRI LANKA, COLOMBIA, AND ETHIOPIA DEVELOP FAR BETTER THAN THE AVERAGE KID WHO'S ACTUALLY *RAISED* IN THOSE COUNTRIES.

PHYSICALLY BETTER

MENTALLY BETTER

PISA TEST SCORE

WITHIN THE FIRST WORLD, EFFORTS TO BOOST IQ ARE PRETTY DISAPPOINTING.

WHILE MANY INTERVENTIONS RAISE IQ, GAINS NORMALLY "FADE OUT" IN A FEW YEARS.

EARLY ADOPTION BY HIGH-IQ FAMILIES BOOSTS *CHILDREN'S* IQs...

BUT EVEN THESE GAINS VANISH BY ADULTHOOD.

MOVING KIDS FROM THE THIRD WORLD TO THE FIRST, IN CONTRAST, HAS A *BIG* AND *LASTING* EFFECT ON IQ.

MOST IMPRESSIVE, A MASSIVE STUDY OF SWEDISH CONSCRIPTS FINDS THAT RECRUITS ADOPTED AS INFANTS FROM THIRD-WORLD COUNTRIES HAVE MUCH HIGHER IQS THAN THE AVERAGE PERSON IN THEIR COUNTRY OF BIRTH.

GROWING UP IN SWEDEN WIPES OUT AT LEAST 40% OF THE INTERNATIONAL IQ CHASM!

BUT CAN WE LEGITIMATELY USE INTERNATIONAL *ADOPTION* TO ESTIMATE THE EFFECTS OF *IMMIGRATION?*

YES, AT LEAST FOR IQ. TO REPEAT: ADOPTION *WITHIN* THE FIRST WORLD HAS LITTLE LASTING EFFECT ON IQ. THAT'S A STANDARD FINDING IN BEHAVIORAL GENETICS.

SO WHEN WE SEE BIG IQ GAINS FOR INTERNATIONAL ADOPTEES, THE KEY INGREDIENT ISN'T THE SPECIFIC FAMILY THAT'S RAISING THEM. IT'S THE KIND OF COUNTRY THEY'RE BEING RAISED *IN*.

PARENTS AROUND THE WORLD LOVE THEIR CHILDREN, BUT LOVE IS NOT ENOUGH. GROWING UP IN WELL-FED, HEALTHY, HIGH-TECH COUNTRIES RESCUES HUMAN BEINGS FROM PHYSICAL *AND* MENTAL STUNTING.

10 Years later

NURTURE'S EFFECT ON IQ LOOKS LIKE THIS MOUNTAIN. THE BIG PLATEAU IS THE FIRST WORLD; AS LONG AS YOU'RE AT THE TOP, YOUR PRECISE LOCATION DOESN'T MUCH MATTER. THE SLOPES ARE THE THIRD WORLD; YOU HAVE LOTS OF ROOM TO RISE UNTIL YOU REACH THE TOP.

AND AS WE'VE SEEN, THE TOP HAS PLENTY OF ROOM FOR EVERYONE.

UPSHOT: OPEN BORDERS WILL BE **GREAT** FOR HUMAN INTELLIGENCE. THE MORE IQ MATTERS, THE MORE YOU SHOULD **WANT** OPEN BORDERS. IT'S PERVERSE TO EXCLUDE PEOPLE "BECAUSE THEIR IQ IS TOO LOW" WHEN EXCLUSION **CAUSES** THEIR IQ TO BE LOW!

IMMIGRATION RESTRICTIONS STUNT THE BRAINPOWER OF THE NEXT GENERATION AS THEY DEPRIVE THE CURRENT GENERATION OF THE OPPORTUNITY TO USE ALL THE BRAINPOWER IT'S GOT.

FREEDOM IS A PRECIOUS THING.

WHEN PEOPLE DEFEND IMMIGRATION RESTRICTIONS IN FREEDOM'S NAME, I SYMPATHIZE.

BUT WHEN YOU CALMLY QUANTIFY THE THREAT IMMIGRANTS POSE TO OUR FREEDOM, THERE'S LITTLE TO SEE. THE THREAT OUR LAWS POSE TO *THEIR* FREEDOM, IN CONTRAST, IS SADLY REAL.

OPEN BORDERS WON'T DESTROY OUR FREEDOM.

IT'S GOING TO BRING FREEDOM TO ALL HUMANITY.

CHAPTER 6
KEYHOLE SOLUTIONS

IN EARLIER TIMES, SURGERY WAS A TRULY HORRIFYING AFFAIR.

YOU MAY EXPERIENCE SOME DISCOMFORT IN THE PARTS OF YOU THAT STAY ATTACHED.

DOCTORS ATTACKED THEIR PATIENTS' PROBLEMS WITHOUT WORRYING MUCH ABOUT SIDE EFFECTS OR RECOVERY TIME.

STOP SQUIRMING!

MODERN MEDICINE, HOWEVER, FAVORS "MINIMALLY INVASIVE," OR "KEYHOLE" SURGERY.

LAPAROSCOPIC CAMERA

SURGICAL INCISION

THE IDEA IS SIMPLE: THE DOCTOR MAKES THE *TINIEST* INCISION *NECESSARY* TO FIX THE PATIENT'S AILMENT. WHY? TO *MINIMIZE* SURGERY'S COLLATERAL DAMAGE.

"FIRST DO NO HARM," RIGHT?

AMPUTATION IS A PHENOMENALLY EFFECTIVE TREATMENT, BUT YOU SHOULD ONLY USE IT AS A LAST RESORT!

THE SAME PRINCIPLE HOLDS IN PUBLIC POLICY. WHILE DRACONIAN ENFORCEMENT OF BYZANTINE REGULATIONS IS ONE WAY TO SOLVE SOCIAL ILLS, THERE'S ALMOST ALWAYS A "KEYHOLE" ALTERNATIVE THAT ADDRESSES THE SAME PROBLEM MORE CHEAPLY AND HUMANELY.

PROBLEM: AIR POLLUTION

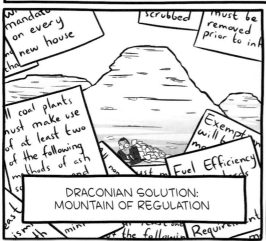

DRACONIAN SOLUTION: MOUNTAIN OF REGULATION

KEYHOLE SOLUTION: TAX POLLUTION

PROBLEM: LOW-INCOME HOUSING SHORTAGE

DRACONIAN SOLUTION: "URBAN RENEWAL"

KEYHOLE SOLUTION: HOUSING VOUCHERS

THIS IS ESPECIALLY TRUE FOR IMMIGRATION. DESPITE THE IMMENSE DIVERSITY OF COMPLAINTS ABOUT IMMIGRATION, ALMOST EVERYONE FAVORS THE **SAME** REMEDY: STRICTER IMMIGRATION CONTROL.

KICK 'EM OUT AND KEEP 'EM OUT!

IMMIGRATION RESTRICTIONS ARE TRULY A SOLUTION IN SEARCH OF A PROBLEM. OR, AS THE OLD SAYING GOES:

WHEN YOUR ONLY TOOL IS A HAMMER, EVERYTHING LOOKS LIKE A NAIL.

PROBLEM: MASS POVERTY

SOLUTION: RESTRICT IMMIGRATION

PROBLEM: FISCAL COLLAPSE

SOLUTION: RESTRICT IMMIGRATION

PROBLEM: CULTURAL DISINTEGRATION

SOLUTION: *RESTRICT IMMIGRATION*

PROBLEM: THE END OF FREEDOM

SOLUTION: *RESTRICT IMMIGRATION!*

AS YOU KNOW, I THINK POPULAR WORRIES ABOUT IMMIGRATION ARE ABSURDLY EXAGGERATED. ON BALANCE, IMMIGRATION HAS VAST ECONOMIC, FISCAL, CULTURAL, AND POLITICAL *BENEFITS*.

BUT EVEN I'LL GRANT THAT IMMIGRATION HAS OCCASIONAL DOWNSIDES. AND PERHAPS FUTURE RESEARCH WILL SHOW THESE DOWNSIDES ARE MORE COMMON AND SEVERE THAN I'VE BEEN TELLING YOU.

IN ANY CASE, YOU'VE PROBABLY FOUND AT LEAST ONE OF THE LAST FOUR CHAPTERS LESS THAN FULLY CONVINCING. I PICTURE THOUGHTFUL READERS ASKING THEMSELVES, "BUT WHAT ABOUT X? I SAY X IS A *HUGE* PROBLEM!"

INSTEAD OF RETRYING TO CHANGE YOUR MIND, I'M NOW GOING TO ACCEPT, FOR THE SAKE OF ARGUMENT, THE VALIDITY OF *ALL* THE TOP COMPLAINTS ABOUT IMMIGRATION. IN EACH CASE, I PROPOSE KEYHOLE SOLUTIONS— POLICIES THAT SPECIFICALLY ADDRESS YOUR CONCERNS WITHOUT BLANKET RESTRICTIONS ON IMMIGRATION.

AND IF OPEN BORDERS IS EVER GOING TO WIN, REASSURING SKEPTICS IS VITAL. WHEN PUSHING AN IDEA AS RADICAL AS OPEN BORDERS, "YOU'RE WITH US OR AGAINST US!" IS CHILDISH.

CAN OPEN BORDERS AND KEYHOLE SOLUTIONS EXIST? NOT PERFECTLY. BUT IF I CONVINCE YOU BORDERS SHOULD BE 90% OR 95% OR 99% OPEN, THERE'S NO NEED TO DWELL ON OUR LINGERING DISAGREEMENTS.

LET'S START WITH IMMIGRATION'S IMPACT ON WAGES AND EMPLOYMENT. NO MATTER WHAT ECONOMISTS TELL THEM, MOST PEOPLE ARE WORRIED...

ESPECIALLY ABOUT LOWER-SKILL NATIVE WORKERS.

IMMIGRANTS TOOK OUR JOBS!

YEAH! THEY TOOK OUR JOBS!

LOOKING 4WORK

I NEED A JOB

INSTEAD OF RESTRICTING IMMIGRATION, HOWEVER, WHY NOT TRY THE FOLLOWING KEYHOLE SOLUTION?

STEP 1: FREELY WELCOME IMMIGRANTS, BUT CHARGE THEM HIGHER TAXES, AN ADMISSION FEE, OR BOTH.

WELCOME TO AMERICA. THAT'LL BE $1,000.

SURE BEATS HIKING THROUGH THE DESERT, LOW ON WATER.

ENTRY FEE: $1000
FOREIGN SURTAX: 10%

U.S.A Estados Unidos

STEP 2: USE IMMIGRANTS' CONTRIBUTIONS TO **COMPENSATE** NATIVES FOR THEIR LOSSES WITH LOWER TAXES, BETTER SERVICES, OR BOTH.

IMMIGRANTS PAID OUR TAXES!

Tax Bill: $0.00

Tax Bill: $0.00

YEAH! THEY PAID OUR TAXES!

NOTICE HOW THIS KEYHOLE SOLUTION WORKS. INSTEAD OF USING ECONOMIC FEARS AS AN EXCUSE FOR CONVENTIONAL IMMIGRATION RESTRICTIONS, WE TAILOR A *SPECIFIC* SOLUTION FOR THE *SPECIFIC* COMPLAINT.

IF IMMIGRATION HURTS LOW-SKILLED NATIVES' TAKE-HOME PAY, THERE'S STILL NO NEED TO EXCLUDE OR DEPORT THEM.

INSTEAD, WHY NOT SIMPLY USE SOME OF THE IMMIGRANTS' GAINS...

...TO OFFSET THE NATIVES' LOSSES?

WAIT, HOW IS THIS BETTER THAN JUST KEEPING FOREIGNERS OUT?

BECAUSE IT HANDLES THE NATIVES' TROUBLES *WITHOUT* DESTROYING THE VAST BENEFITS OF IMMIGRATION! SINCE IMMIGRATION ENRICHES THE WORLD, PILES OF NEW WEALTH REMAIN *AFTER* WE COMPENSATE NATIVES WHO LOSE.

I CAN'T BELIEVE YOU'RE SAYING THIS.

YOU CLAIM TO CARE ABOUT IMMIGRANTS, BUT YOUR "KEYHOLE SOLUTION" IS *SO* UNFAIR TO US.

YEAH, WHY SHOULD IMMIGRANTS STRUGGLING TO WORK THEIR WAY OUT OF POVERTY HAVE TO SUBSIDIZE THE LIFESTYLE OF AMERICANS WHO LIVE FAR BETTER THAN WE DO?

I COMPLETELY AGREE. MY KEYHOLE SOLUTION *IS* UNFAIR TO IMMIGRANTS.

BUT, IT'S FAR *LESS* UNFAIR THAN SAYING YOU CAN'T COME AT ALL. AND SADLY, THAT'S OUR STATUS QUO.

ISN'T "IMMIGRANTS ARE WELCOME, BUT HAVE TO PAY EXTRA TAXES" FAIRER TO YOU THAN "KEEP OUT"?

KEYHOLE SOLUTIONS FOR FISCAL FEARS ARE EVEN MORE OBVIOUS. WORRIED ABOUT IMMIGRANTS WHO COST MORE IN SERVICES THAN THEY PAY IN TAXES?

Medicare

free idealistic public educator

Social Security

EXCLUSION AND DEPORTATION ARE THE KNEE-JERK SOLUTIONS...

...BUT THERE'S A CHEAPER, MORE HUMANE ALTERNATIVE.

STEP 1: RESTRICT IMMIGRANTS' ELIGIBILITY FOR FREE AND SUBSIDIZED GOVERNMENT SERVICES.

BURSAR'S OFFICE

IN-STATE TUITION: $8,000

OUT-OF-STATE TUITION: $15,000

NON-CITIZEN TUITION: $25,000

STEP 2: THERE IS NO STEP 2.

IMMIGRANTS' "NET FISCAL EFFECT" IS NOT A FIXED VALUE, LIKE PLANCK'S CONSTANT. IT DEPENDS ON OUR LAWS— AND THOSE LAWS CAN BE REVISED.

IF YOU THINK IMMIGRANTS ARE SUCKING NATIVE TAXPAYERS DRY, WHY NOT TARGET THE BENEFITS THEY RECEIVE RATHER THAN IMMIGRANTS THEMSELVES? AS CATO'S ALEX NOWRASTEH OFTEN SAYS...

"LET'S BUILD A WALL AROUND THE WELFARE STATE, INSTEAD OF THE COUNTRY!"

HOW UNFAIR! I PAY THE SAME TAXES AS EVERYONE ELSE, SO I SHOULD GET THE SAME SERVICES, TOO.

TO WHICH I CAN AGAIN REPLY...

RESTRICTING IMMIGRANTS' BENEFITS IS CLEARLY A LOT *LESS* UNFAIR THAN SAYING IMMIGRANTS CAN'T COME AT ALL.

IN ANY CASE, IF AN IMMIGRANT REALLY *IS* A FISCAL BURDEN, THEN HE NORMALLY *DOESN'T* "PAY THE SAME TAXES AS EVERYONE ELSE." PERHAPS IT WOULD GENUINELY BE FAIRER TO...

LIMIT IMMIGRANTS TO THE MOST VITAL SERVICES...

VACCINES! USE THEM, FOR GOD'S SAKE.

IMPOSE A WAITING PERIOD...

Ticket # 662,607,009

OR REQUIRE IMMIGRANTS TO PAY, SAY, $100K IN TAXES BEFORE THEY CAN APPLY FOR BENEFITS.

ELIGIBLE!

$100,000
$90,000
$80,000
$70,000
$60,000
$50,000
$40,000

WHATEVER THE RIGHT BALANCE, CONCERNED TAXPAYERS CAN READILY SOLVE THEIR PROBLEMS WITHOUT RESTRICTING MIGRATION.

BUT PERHAPS CULTURE IS MORE ABOUT WHAT YOU *DO* THAN WHAT YOU *KNOW*.

WORRIED ABOUT CRIME? YOU COULD EXCLUDE INDIVIDUALS WITH CRIMINAL RECORDS—REGARDLESS OF THEIR TEST SCORES.

EVEN MORE OBVIOUSLY, THERE'S NO REASON FOR THE LAW TO TREAT "THIS IS OKAY IN MY CULTURE" AS AN EXCUSE FOR CHILD ABUSE OR OTHER BARBARITIES.

INTERNATIONAL DAY *of* ZERO TOLERANCE *for* FEMALE GENITAL MUTILATION

February 6

SOME COUNTRIES, LIKE FRANCE, TRY TO PROTECT THEIR CULTURE BY BANNING "UN-FRENCH" OUTFITS LIKE BURKAS AND BURKINIS.

DOES THIS QUALIFY AS A KEYHOLE SOLUTION? YES, IF STOPPING MUSLIM IMMIGRATION IS THE ALTERNATIVE.

ISLAMOPHOBIC?

SURE, BUT IT'S FAR *LESS* ISLAMOPHOBIC THAN SAYING WE CAN'T COME AT ALL.

Qu'est que vous pensez de mon Burkini?!

What do you think of my BURKINI

BUT WHAT IF YOU DON'T SHARE MY OPTIMISM?

WHAT IF YOU'RE CONVINCED MUSLIM AND WESTERN CULTURE ARE IRRECONCILABLE?

THAT WE'RE WELL ON OUR WAY TO THE DEMOGRAPHIC POINT OF NO RETURN?

I'VE STILL GOT A KEYHOLE SOLUTION: INSTEAD OF SLASHING MUSLIM IMMIGRATION, WHY NOT RAISE *NON*-MUSLIM IMMIGRATION?

MUSLIMS ARE 24% OF THE WORLD POPULATION. IF THEY WERE EVENLY DISTRIBUTED THROUGHOUT THE WORLD, THEY WOULDN'T BE THE DOMINANT CULTURE ANYWHERE.

THE SAME GOES FOR *ANY* DISCONCERTING DEMOGRAPHIC.

WORRIED YOUR MALE/FEMALE RATIO IS GETTING TOO HIGH? INSTEAD OF EXCLUDING MEN...

WHY NOT JUST ADMIT MORE WOMEN?

SIMILARLY, INSTEAD OF TRYING TO KEEP OUT FUTURE DEMOCRATS, WHY NOT WELCOME MORE FUTURE REPUBLICANS TO BALANCE THEM OUT?

FINALLY, IF YOU'RE WORRIED IMMIGRANTS ARE GOING TO TAKE AWAY OUR FREEDOM, THERE'S ANOTHER SIMPLE TWO-STEP KEYHOLE SOLUTION.

STEP 1: AWARD CITIZENSHIP CAUTIOUSLY.

STEP 2: THERE IS NO STEP 2.

YOU COULD JUST MAKE IMMIGRANTS WAIT YEARS AND YEARS TO NATURALIZE, SO THEY HAVE AMPLE TIME TO LEARN TO LOVE OUR POLITICAL IDEALS.

OR YOU COULD REQUIRE IMMIGRANTS TO PASS A *RIGOROUS* CIVICS TEST TO GAIN CITIZENSHIP.

UNFAIR? MAYBE. BUT REMEMBER, MOST IMMIGRANTS ARE SEEKING OPPORTUNITY AND FREEDOM FOR THEIR FAMILIES, NOT THE SUBTLE SATISFACTION OF VOTING.

BUT ISN'T THIS JUST PIE IN THE SKY?

ARE ANY OF THESE KEYHOLE SOLUTIONS POLITICALLY POSSIBLE?

ABSOLUTELY, BECAUSE WHAT *EXISTS* IS POSSIBLE. PLENTY OF THESE POLICIES ARE ALREADY ON THE BOOKS!

FOREIGN TOURISTS, MOST OBVIOUSLY, CAN'T VOTE AND ARE INELIGIBLE FOR ALMOST ALL GOVERNMENT BENEFITS.

I HAD APPLE PIE AND A HOT DOG AND I WENT TO DISNEY AND CAN I PLEASE PLEASE PLEASE VOTE IN A CITY COUNCIL ELECTION? MY FRIENDS BACK IN SLOVAKIA WILL BE SO JEALOUS!

YOU PEOPLE NEED NETFLIX.

THE SAME GOES FOR INTERNATIONAL STUDENTS.

DON'T FORGET—THEY ALMOST ALWAYS PAY OUT-OF-STATE TUITION. NO WONDER PUBLIC COLLEGES LOVE THEM!

IN 1996, SIMILARLY, BILL CLINTON'S WELFARE REFORM RESTRICTED FEDERAL WELFARE BENEFITS FOR IMMIGRANTS.

Welfare to Work

WANT TO COLLECT TANF, SNAP, OR MEDICAID? THERE'S A FIVE-YEAR WAITING PERIOD (THOUGH SOME STATES FUND WHAT THE FEDS WON'T).

HAPPY TO HELP.

JUST FILL OUT THESE FORMS AND YOU'LL HEAR BACK FROM US NEXT DECADE.

Medicaid

Naturalization Eligibility Worksheet

LEGAL IMMIGRANTS NORMALLY HAVE TO WAIT FIVE YEARS JUST TO *APPLY* FOR CITIZENSHIP.

REALISTICALLY, THEN, EVEN IMMIGRANTS DYING TO VOTE IN U.S. ELECTIONS HAVE TO WAIT SIX OR SEVEN YEARS TO DO SO.

ANYONE WHO CARES ABOUT IMMIGRATION NEEDS TO TAKE THIS BIBLE STORY TO HEART. IF WE CAN CRAFT A KEYHOLE SOLUTION THAT PERSUADES A COUNTRY TO WELCOME *ONE* EXTRA IMMIGRANT, WE'VE DONE A GREAT GOOD.

BUT KEYHOLE SOLUTIONS ALSO TEACH A DEEPER LESSON: THE OPPONENTS OF IMMIGRATION KNOW *WHAT* THEY WANT TO DO LONG BEFORE THEY KNOW *WHY*.

I'VE SAID IT BEFORE AND I'LL SAY IT AGAIN: IMMIGRATION RESTRICTIONS ARE A SOLUTION IN SEARCH OF A PROBLEM.

"HOW CAN IMMIGRATION RESTRICTIONS HANDLE PROBLEM X?" IS SIMPLY A *BAD QUESTION*.

IT MAKES FAR MORE SENSE TO ASK: "WHAT'S THE CHEAPEST, MOST HUMANE WAY TO HANDLE PROBLEM X?"

REFRAMING THE QUESTION MAY NOT TAKE YOU ALL THE WAY TO OPEN BORDERS.

BUT YOU'LL NEVER GO BACK TO THE INTELLECTUAL LAZINESS OF "KICK 'EM OUT AND KEEP 'EM OUT."

UTILITARIANISM

J.S. Mill

MAXIMIZE THE SUM OF HUMAN HAPPINESS.

EGALITARIANISM

John Rawls

INEQUALITIES MUST BENEFIT THE WORST-OFF.

LIBERTARIANISM

Robert Nozick

"FROM EACH AS HE CHOOSES, TO EACH AS HE IS CHOSEN."

COST-BENEFIT ANALYSIS

Richard Posner

MAXIMIZE THE TOTAL VALUE OF SOCIAL RESOURCES.

MERITOCRACY

Lee Kuan Yew

THE BEST JOB FOR THE BEST PERSON.

CHRISTIANITY

Jesus

"DO UNTO OTHERS AS YOU WOULD HAVE OTHERS DO UNTO YOU."

KANTIANISM

Immanuel Kant

TREAT EVERY PERSON AS AN END IN HIMSELF, NEVER AS A MERE MEANS!

VERY WELL. I'LL TRY TO RECONSTRUCT YOUR POSITION.

AH, YES. OPEN BORDERS WILL INCREASE THE SUM OF HUMAN HAPPINESS BY SHARPLY RAISING GLOBAL PRODUCTION...

WHILE REDUCING GLOBAL INEQUALITY.

THE LATTER'S IMPORTANT BECAUSE A DOLLAR MEANS FAR MORE TO A BEGGAR THAN A BILLIONAIRE.

EXACTLY! OPEN BORDERS ENRICHES THE WORLD BY ENDING MANDATORY DISCRIMINATION AGAINST THE GLOBAL POOR.

THOUGH THERE ARE INDUBITABLY SOME OFFSETTING EFFECTS, A GOOD UTILITARIAN MUST WEIGH THEM BY THEIR SEVERITY AND PROBABILITY. NONE ARE PLAUSIBLY WORTH TRILLIONS OF DOLLARS PER YEAR.

SPLENDID!

YOUR TURN, RAWLS.

UNLIKE MILLS, I ASSIGN SPECIAL ETHICAL IMPORTANCE TO THE WELL-BEING OF THE *LEAST* FORTUNATE.

INEQUALITIES ARE *ONLY* JUSTIFIED IF THEY REDOUND TO THE BENEFIT OF THE WORST-OFF.

WE RAWLSIANS NORMALLY PRESUME THE "WORST-OFF" ARE RELATIVELY POOR PEOPLE IN THE FIRST WORLD. BUT ON SOBER REFLECTION, THE GLOBAL POOR ARE IN A FAR MORE DESPERATE POSITION.

DUH.

AND LARGELY BECAUSE OF *MANDATORY* UNEQUAL TREATMENT. OUR LAWS DEPRIVE THE GLOBAL POOR OF THE VERY RIGHTS TO LIVE AND WORK WHERE THEY LIKE.

I'M CONFIDENT WE CAN COMBINE OPEN BORDERS WITH A GENEROUS WELFARE STATE. BUT IF WE HAVE TO CHOOSE ONE...

...EGALITARIAN PRINCIPLES ALMOST *COMPEL* ME TO CHOOSE...

OPEN BORDERS.

COST-BENEFIT ANALYSIS

WAIT, ISN'T THIS JUST THE SAME AS UTILITARIANISM.?

NOPE. UTILITARIANS WANT TO MAXIMIZE HAPPINESS. COST-BENEFIT ANALYSIS MAXIMIZES RESOURCES' *DOLLAR* VALUE.

"A DOLLAR MEANS MORE TO A POOR MAN THAN A RICH MAN".? *MEH*.

SO I'VE CERTAINLY GOT ONE *LESS* REASON TO SUPPORT OPEN BORDERS THAN A SOFTIE LIKE MILL.

PLEASE, SIR, I WANT SOME MORE.

BAH!

STILL, IT'S DAMN HARD TO USE COST-BENEFIT ANALYSIS TO ARGUE *AGAINST* DOUBLING GLOBAL GDP!

WE SHOULD KEEP A CLOSE EYE ON ALL OF IMMIGRATION'S DOWNSIDE RISKS. BUT THE SIZE OF THE DOWNSIDES WOULD HAVE TO BE ASTRONOMICAL FOR THE COSTS OF OPEN BORDERS TO OUTWEIGH ITS BENEFITS.

SO....?

WITH ALL DUE CAUTION... OPEN BORDERS.

YOU'RE GOING TO TELL ME THAT IMMIGRATION LAWS TREAT FOREIGNERS AS "MERE MEANS"?

EXACTLY. LET'S REVIEW A CLASSIC KANTIAN THOUGHT EXPERIMENT.

OI!!

THE POLICE ACCIDENTALLY ARREST THE WRONG MAN FOR MURDER.

STRING HIM UP!

STRING HIM UP!!

STRING HIM UP!!!

BY THE TIME THE AUTHORITIES DISCOVER THEIR MISTAKE, AN ANGRY LYNCH MOB HAS FORMED.

OI.

THE MORAL DILEMMA: SHOULD THE STATE SENTENCE AN INNOCENT MAN TO PRISON TO PLACATE THE MOB?

I STAND BY THE TEXTBOOK KANTIAN ANSWER:

THE MAN HAS DONE NO WRONG. COME WHAT MAY, THERE IS A MORAL IMPERATIVE *NOT* TO PUNISH HIM.

SUPPOSE THE PUNISHMENT WERE NOT PRISON, BUT BANISHMENT TO THE THIRD WORLD?

IT CHANGES NOTHING. PERSONALLY, I'D RATHER SPEND A FEW YEARS IN JAIL...

THEN HOW CAN IT BE MORALLY PERMISSIBLE TO SO BANISH BILLIONS OF HUMAN BEINGS WHOSE ONLY "CRIME" IS BEING BORN IN THE WRONG COUNTRY?

YOUR ANALOGY IS TROUBLING, BUT NOT FULLY CONVINCING.

COULDN'T YOU JUST AS EASILY ACCUSE ME OF "BANISHING" STRANGERS FROM MY HOUSE?

I KNOW WHERE YOU'RE COMING FROM—AND YOU'RE HARDLY ALONE. CONSERVATIVES ARE ESPECIALLY FOND OF THIS OBJECTION.

TO EVALUATE IT, LET'S RETURN TO MIKE HUEMER'S "STARVING MARVIN" HYPOTHETICAL.

MARVIN TRIES TO BUY FOOD. SAM STOPS HIM. MORALLY SPEAKING, WHAT DO YOU TWO HAVE TO SAY FOR YOURSELVES?

I'M CONFUSED. I THOUGHT YOUR COUNTRY HAD A MARKET ECONOMY BASED ON PRIVATE PROPERTY.

IT DOES.

THEN HOW IS SHOPPING IN A PRIVATE STORE "TRESPASSING"?

YOUR TRESPASSING STORY ONLY MAKES SENSE IF THE PEOPLE OF YOUR COUNTRY COLLECTIVELY OWN THE WHOLE COUNTRY.

IF WHAT APPEARS TO BE PRIVATE PROPERTY RIGHTFULLY BELONGS TO SOCIETY AS A WHOLE...

THERE IS A NAME FOR THAT VIEW. THE LAST TIME I CHECKED, CONSERVATIVES WERE NONE TOO FOND OF IT.

SOCIALISM.

AND IF YOU REALLY THINK SOCIETY AS A WHOLE RIGHTFULLY OWNS THE WHOLE COUNTRY...

THEN ISN'T SOCIETY WITHIN ITS RIGHTS TO DICTATE YOUR JOB, YOUR RELIGION, AND EVERYTHING ELSE?

DIG FASTER, PROFESSOR!

GOTT IM HIMMEL!

LOVE IT OR LEAVE IT!

IF YOU DARE...

V. I. Lenin

WHO WANTS TO BITE THAT BULLET?

IN RECENT YEARS, IMMIGRATION HAS BECOME A DIVISIVE PARTISAN ISSUE.

NAZIS!

TRAITORS!

LEFT-WING SUPPORT FOR IMMIGRATION HAS SWELLED—BUT SO HAS RIGHT-WING OPPOSITION.

OPEN BORDERS MEETUP '19

WHILE I'M DELIGHTED TO SEE SO MANY ON THE LEFT COMING AROUND, THIS POLARIZATION SCARES ME.

I DON'T WANT TO SEE A PRO-IMMIGRATION PARTY FIGHT AN ANTI-IMMIGRATION PARTY.

TAKEN LITERALLY, CITIZENISM IS VULNERABLE TO DEVASTATING MORAL COUNTER-EXAMPLES.

AMERICA ABOVE *ALL* ELSE.? WHAT IF THE U.S. COULD END FOREIGN HUNGER FOR A DOLLAR?

AMERICA ABOVE *ALL* ELSE.? WHAT IF THE U.S. COULD ENRICH ITSELF BY ENSLAVING CANADA.?

BUT WHEN PRESSED, CITIZENISTS NORMALLY TONE DOWN THEIR POSITION.

"WE'RE PUTTING THE AMERICAN PEOPLE FIRST AGAIN ON TRADE, ON IMMIGRATION, ON FOREIGN POLICY."

"BOTH OUR FRIENDS AND OUR ENEMIES PUT THEIR COUNTRIES ABOVE OURS AND WE, *WHILE BEING FAIR TO THEM*, MUST START DOING THE SAME."

SO WHAT'S WRONG WITH A SUITABLY TONED-DOWN VERSION OF CITIZENISM.?

TO START: CITIZENISTS' COMPLAINTS ABOUT INTERNATIONAL TRADE ARE DEEPLY CONFUSED.

WHEN FOREIGNERS SELL AMERICANS CHEAP STUFF, THEY'RE NOT "TAKING ADVANTAGE OF US," THEY'RE *SERVING* US.

FOR AMERICANS, THE ONLY THING BETTER THAN CHEAP FOREIGN PRODUCTS IS *FREE* FOREIGN PRODUCTS!

SERIOUSLY, IF WE GOT LIMITLESS IMPORTS IN EXCHANGE FOR *ZERO* EXPORTS, WOULDN'T THAT BE IDEAL FOR US?

AND, ECONOMICALLY SPEAKING, WHAT IS IMMIGRATION? INTERNATIONAL TRADE IN LABOR!

WHILE PROGRESS ALWAYS HURTS SOMEONE, THE SECRET OF MASS CONSUMPTION IS MASS PRODUCTION.

BUY 1, GET 16,180 FREE!

SALE! 128% OFF!

I'VE SAID IT BEFORE AND I'LL SAY IT AGAIN. IF YOU KNOW NOTHING ELSE ABOUT ECONOMICS, KNOW *THIS*.

OKAY, SO WHAT'S THE BEST ARGUMENT *AGAINST* OPEN BORDERS?

SKEPTIC

YEAH!

GREAT QUESTION!

THE PRECAUTIONARY PRINCIPLE.

NO MATTER HOW PROMISING A RADICAL SOCIAL CHANGE SOUNDS, THERE'S ALWAYS A CHANCE IT ENDS IN DISASTER.

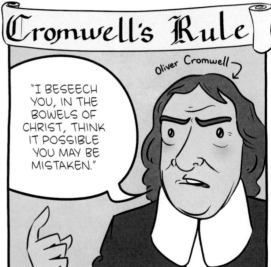

Cromwell's Rule

Oliver Cromwell

"I BESEECH YOU, IN THE BOWELS OF CHRIST, THINK IT POSSIBLE YOU MAY BE MISTAKEN."

IT'S A WEIGHTY ARGUMENT. BUT IN THIS CASE, IT'S OVERRATED.

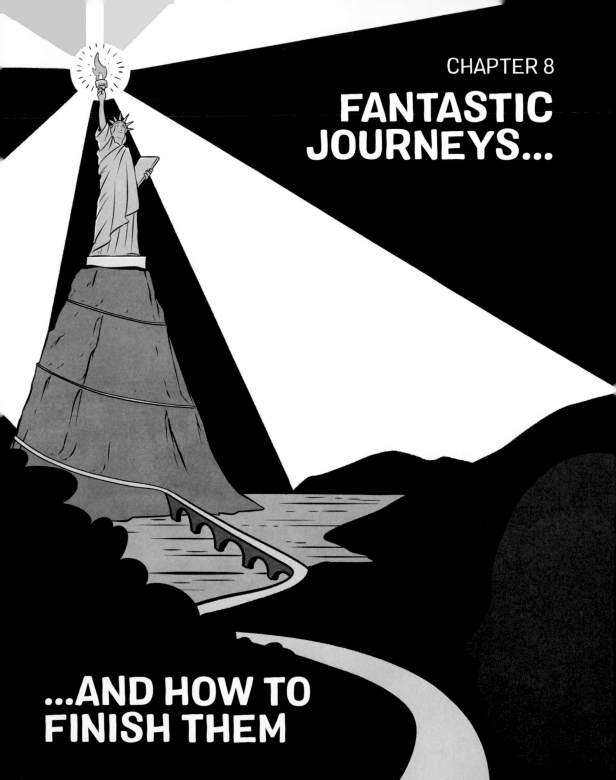

CHAPTER 8
FANTASTIC JOURNEYS...

...AND HOW TO FINISH THEM

IN THE CONVENTIONAL FRAME, ALLOWING IMMIGRATION IS AN ACT OF NATIONAL CHARITY.

UNLESS THE IMMIGRANT IS A BRAIN SURGEON, ROCKET SCIENTIST, OR SUPERMODEL, WE'RE DOING HIM A FAVOR OUT OF THE KINDNESS OF OUR HEARTS.

WHICH QUICKLY RAISES TWO AWKWARD QUESTIONS.

HOW MANY IMMIGRANTS CAN WE AFFORD TO TAKE?

AND SHOULDN'T WE TAKE CARE OF OUR *OWN* PEOPLE FIRST?

TRUE, WE CAN'T CHANGE PEOPLE'S MINDS OVERNIGHT.

THAT'S WHY FOLKS LIKE JOSE ANTONIO VARGAS ARE SO EAGER TO LAUNCH A DIALOGUE.

Pulitzer Prize Winner

Filipino DREAMer

Founder of Define America

Fearless

"I'M MORE THAN WILLING TO GO TO PLACES AND TALK TO PEOPLE WHO BELIEVE THAT I AM AN ILLEGAL ALIEN WHO DESERVES TO BE JAILED."

"I WANT TO LOOK THEM IN THE EYE AND SAY, 'WHAT MAKES YOU THINK I'M ANY DIFFERENT FROM YOU?'"

IF OPEN BORDERS WINS, IT WILL WIN GRADUALLY, ONE MIND AT A TIME.

OPEN BORDERS

Pass the DREAM

PERHAPS WITH THE HELP OF SOME KEYHOLE SOLUTIONS TO SOOTHE SKEPTICS' NERVES.

AND EVEN IF OPEN BORDERS *NEVER* WINS, THE IDEAL CAN STILL SERVE AS OUR MORAL COMPASS.

WHILE THE TOPIC OF THIS BOOK IS *GLOBAL* OPEN BORDERS, I'VE LAVISHED ATTENTION ON U.S. IMMIGRATION POLICY.

BECAUSE YOU HATE AMERICA.?

NOPE. AND I'M NOT SINGLING THE U.S. OUT FOR CRITICISM.

I'M PREACHING TO EVERY COUNTRY ON EARTH.

I DWELL ON THE U.S. BECAUSE:

THE U.S. IS MIGRANTS' FAVORITE DESTINATION.

AS THE WORLD'S LEADING NATION, THE U.S. IS A MODEL FOR THE REST OF THE WORLD.

THERE'S TONS OF RELEVANT RESEARCH— AND A VAST AUDIENCE EAGER TO LEARN MORE.

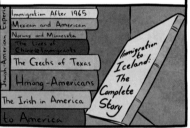

Jewish American Experie

Immigration After 1965

Mexican and American

Norway and Minnesota

The Lives of Chinese Immigrants

The Czechs of Texas

Hmong-Americans

The Irish in America

to America

Immigration to Iceland: The Complete Story

THE U.S. HAS A GLORIOUS HISTORY OF OPEN IMMIGRATION.

AND DESPITE MAJOR LAPSES, WELCOMING IMMIGRANTS TO OUR "SHINING CITY ON A HILL" REMAINS CENTRAL TO AMERICANS' NATIONAL IDENTITY.

WHICH MAKES MY NEXT QUESTION ALL THE MORE AWKWARD.

WHAT THE HELL IS THE ARGUMENT AGAINST OPEN BORDERS WITH CANADA?

THE ONLY THING THAT STANDS IN THE WAY OF OPENING THIS BORDER IS SHEER POLITICAL APATHY.

BUT SO FAR, SHEER POLITICAL APATHY HAS EFFORTLESSLY HELD ITS GROUND. PATHETIC— AND DISCOURAGING!

THERE IS NO ARGUMENT. GIVING AMERICANS AND CANADIANS FULL FREEDOM TO LIVE AND WORK IN EITHER COUNTRY IS A CLEAR-CUT NO-BRAINER WIN-WIN!

BEFORE YOU GIVE UP, THOUGH, CONSIDER THIS:

IN 1945, EUROPE LAY IN RUINS.

THE BLOODTHIRSTY NATIONALISM OF WORLD WAR I HAD INSPIRED AN EVEN BLOODIER SEQUEL.

IT WOULD HAVE BEEN EASY FOR CONTEMPORARIES TO CONCLUDE THAT SAVAGE NATIONALISM IS BAKED INTO HUMAN NATURE.

AT THE TIME, IF ANYONE PREDICTED THAT EUROPE WAS ABOUT TO TURN ITS BACK ON WAR AND CREATE A PAN-EUROPEAN ZONE FOR NOT ONLY FREE TRADE, BUT FREE MIGRATION...

...THE WHOLE WORLD WOULD'VE GRIMLY GUFFAWED.

French Polynesia Nuclear Test Zone

WELL, AT LEAST WE KNOW THERE WON'T BE A WORLD WAR IV.

THE GREAT POWERS OF EUROPE SET ASIDE THEIR DIFFERENCES AND MADE A LASTING PEACE.

NOW GUESS WHAT HAPPENED...

WESTERN EUROPE BUILT A VAST FREE-TRADE ZONE...

WHICH PEACEFULLY EXPANDED BOTH NORTH AND EAST.

"FREE TRADE" SLOWLY CAME TO INCLUDE NOT JUST GOODS, BUT LABOR.

NOW, WITH TOKEN EXCEPTIONS, EVERY CITIZEN OF THIS VAST CULTURALLY DIVERSE FREE-TRADE ZONE IS FREE TO LIVE AND WORK ANYWHERE WITHIN IT!

EVENTS LIKE BREXIT DON'T SHOW THAT EUROPEANS ARE "WAKING UP" TO GLARING DOWNSIDES OF IMMIGRATION.

VOTE TO LEAVE THE EU

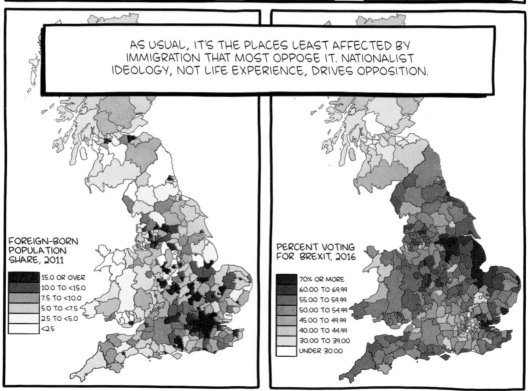

AS USUAL, IT'S THE PLACES LEAST AFFECTED BY IMMIGRATION THAT MOST OPPOSE IT. NATIONALIST IDEOLOGY, NOT LIFE EXPERIENCE, DRIVES OPPOSITION.

FOREIGN-BORN POPULATION SHARE, 2011

15.0 OR OVER
10.0 TO <15.0
7.5 TO <10.0
5.0 TO <7.5
2.5 TO <5.0
<2.5

PERCENT VOTING FOR BREXIT, 2016

70% OR MORE
60.00 TO 69.99
55.00 TO 59.99
50.00 TO 54.99
45.00 TO 49.99
40.00 TO 44.99
30.00 TO 39.00
UNDER 30.00

WHILE U.S. OPPOSITION TO IMMIGRATION REMAINS HIGH...

IT HAS SHARPLY FALLEN SINCE ITS PEAK TWO DECADES AGO.

SUPPORT FOR *MORE* IMMIGRATION, STUCK AT SINGLE DIGITS FOR THIRTY YEARS...

AMERICANS' PREFERENCES FOR U.S. IMMIGRATION LEVELS, 1965–2018

PRESENT LEVEL

INCREASED

DECREASED

...HAS QUADRUPLED. OVER A QUARTER OF THE POPULATION NOW FAVORS LIBERALIZATION.

AND SINCE THE FOREIGN-BORN POPULATION SHARE WAS STEADILY RISING DURING THIS PERIOD, THE SURGE OF SUPPORT FOR *INCREASED* IMMIGRATION IS EVEN MORE IMPRESSIVE THAN IT LOOKS!

CRITICS OFTEN DISMISS OPEN BORDERS AS YET ANOTHER CRAZY IVORY TOWER PLAN TO REMAKE SOCIETY.

"ALL CITIZENS WILL BE REQUIRED TO CHANGE THEIR UNDERWEAR EVERY HALF-HOUR. UNDERWEAR WILL BE WORN ON THE OUTSIDE SO WE CAN CHECK!"

THE CRITICS ARE WRONG. OPEN BORDERS LEAVES OUR FUNDAMENTAL INSTITUTIONS UNTOUCHED. IT JUST REPEALS A FEW CRIPPLING REGULATIONS.

OPEN BORDERS GENERALIZES A PRINCIPLE THAT'S BEEN BUILDING JUST AND PROSPEROUS LANDS FOR CENTURIES: EQUALITY OF OPPORTUNITY.

GIVING EVERY HUMAN BEING THE CHANCE TO EXERCISE HIS TALENTS IS BOTH COMMON DECENCY...

...AND THE HEIGHT OF PRUDENCE.

OPEN BORDERS PRACTICALLY *DEFINES* "WELL-GROUNDED OPTIMISM."

REALIZING THIS FANTASTIC OPPORTUNITY WILL BE A *LONG* JOURNEY.

NOTES

CHAPTER 1:
GLOBAL APARTHEID

p.5, panel 1. This graph uses (a) IMF data for World GDP adjusted for Purchasing Power Parity in international dollars, (b) the CPI to convert international dollars into constant U.S. dollars, and (c) the U.S. Census for global population. Special thanks to Mark J. Perry for performing all calculations.

p.5, panel 2. This graph comes from World Bank Group 2016, p.5.

p.7, panel 3. According to the United Nations, annual migration into OECD countries has ranged from about 4 million in 2000 to about 7 million in 2015. The estimated global migrant population is about 244 million, about 3.3% of global population. In other words, 96.7% of humanity continue to reside in their country of birth. (International Organization for Migration 2017, pps.24, 15). For further information, see Connor et al. 2013.

p.8, panel 2. Clifton 2013. Esipova and Ray 2012 estimates that 600 million globally wish to permanently move to another country, and over a billion wish to seek temporary work abroad. Esipova et al. 2009, 2014, and Esipova 2017 estimate population gain and loss if everyone on Earth migrated to their first-choice destination. Despite the noisiness of the annual estimates, many hundreds of millions clearly desire to move to another country.

p.8, panel 3. According to the last Census (United States Census Bureau 2018a), Los Angeles County has a population density of 2,419 people per square mile. Since the continental United States is 3,119,885 square miles in area, this area would contain about 7.6 billion people, the current world population.

p.8, panel 5.	See especially Clemens et al. forthcoming, Pritchett 2006, pp.18–27, and further discussion in chapter 2 of this book.
p.9, panel 2.	Some commentators favor an expansive definition of "global apartheid" such as "an international system of minority rule whose attributes include: differential access to basic human rights; wealth and power structured by race and place; structural racism, embedded in global economic processes, political institutions and cultural assumptions; and the international practice of double standards that assume inferior rights to be appropriate for certain 'others,' defined by location, origin, race or gender." (Booker and Minter 2001) But others, notably Lant Pritchett, focus on South African apartheid's most distinctive feature: mobility restrictions. "It is said that fish do not know they are swimming in water. The analogy between apartheid and restrictions on labor mobility is almost exact. People are not allowed to live and work where they please." (Pritchett 2006, p.79; see also Howley 2008)

> WATER?
> I DON'T SEE
> ANY WATER!

For a review of the evidence on the strictness and enforcement of immigration laws, see Caplan and Naik 2015, pp.181–3.

p.10, panel 2.	For recent international statistics on illegal (or "irregular") immigration, see International Organization for Migration 2017, pp.20–1.
p.11, panels 1–2.	For further discussion, see Caplan and Naik 2015, pp.184–5, and Caplan 2012a.
p.12, panels 1–2.	For admittedly imperfect estimates of human smuggling fees, see Havocscope 2018. These figures have apparently not been updated since 2014 at the latest; due to inflation, we should expect them to be modestly higher today. Roberts et al. 2010, p.5, reports a lower average Mexican smuggling figure of roughly $2,000 as of 2007.
p.12, panels 3–4.	See Roberts et al. 2013, pp.20–5.
p.13.	For a more academic version of this common-sense ethical argument, see Chang 2003.
p.14, panel 1.	King 1963, p.5.
p.15.	For general discussion of open borders, see Caplan 2012b, Caplan and Naik 2015, Van der Vossen and Brennan 2018, Legrain 2007, Pritchett 2006, and the website openborders.info. Critics occasionally equate "open borders" with "no borders," but these are distinct proposals; an open borders regime could still have border checkpoints, require passports, and so on. The acid test, in my view, is that an open borders regime does not subject foreigners to any mobility restrictions *more stringent than natives face*. Thus, if a foreigner commits a crime warranting incarceration, an open borders regime could impose the lesser punishment of exclusion. Similarly, if a foreigner has a contagious disease warranting quarantine, an open borders regime could impose the lesser precaution of exclusion.
p.16.	For elaboration of these points, see Caplan 2013a.
pp.17–19.	See Huemer 2010 for a full discussion. All quotations from Huemer 2010, pp.431–3.
p.21, panels 1–3.	For brief histories of U.S. immigration policy, see Gjelten 2015, pp.79–135 and Gerber 2011, pp.17–64.
p.21, panel 2.	This image, "The Magic Washer" 1886, is an advertisement for a laundry detergent.

The fine print reads, "The Chinese must go. We have no use for them since we got this wonderful washer."

p.21, panel 4. See Ratiner 2015, pp.1–39 for a short discussion of the life and work of Emma Lazarus, and pp.202–3 for the text of her poem "The New Colossus," mounted inside the lower level of the pedestal of "Liberty Enlightening the World," better known as the Statue of Liberty.

p.22, panel 1. This image, "The Usual Irish Way of Doing Things," shows a drunken Irish terrorist. (Nast 1871)

p.22, panel 2. This image, "Know-Nothing," c.1850, shows Irish and German immigrants stealing a ballot box.

p.22, panel 3. This image, "What We Would Like to See," 1888, shows the expulsion of an Italian "pauper" and a Chinese "coolie."

p.22, panels 4–5. According to the Maddison Project Database 2018, U.S. per-capita GDP (variable identifier cgdppc) overtook the United Kingdom's to become the world's highest by 1830. It has remained at or very near the top ever since, occasionally losing out to Australia and New Zealand in the 19th century, and low-population, oil-rich states beginning in the late 20th century. Total U.S. GDP surpassed the United Kingdom's by 1860, and both China and India's by 1890. Total GDP calculated by multiplying Maddison variable identifiers pop*cgdppc. In World War I, the United States fielded fewer troops than any of the other major powers, but clearly retained vast untapped military potential due to the total size of its economy.

pp.23–24. On the end of America's open borders era, see Gjelten 2015, pp.79–94. For further discussion, see Ngai 1999, Ludmerer 1972, and Parker 1924. Parker, writing almost immediately after the passage of the 1924 Immigration Act, opines, "While it is by far the most drastic immigration statute ever passed by the United States Congress, it is in numerous respects the most humane measure yet devised." He then declares that, "*The main objects* of the new, as of the old, quota law are: first, a sufficient reduction in the volume of immigration to give assurance that the country will not admit more annually than it can accommodate; and, second, making the reduction fall most heavily on the 'new immigration' countries (of southern and eastern Europe), and most lightly on those countries (of western and northern Europe) from which our earlier immigration was principally derived—this in order to give assurance of the more rapid assimilation of those admitted." (Parker 1924, 737-8) Many other prominent voices, including Calvin Coolidge and Secretary of Labor James Davis, openly praised the racial—rather than merely cultural—superiority of the Nordic race. (Ludmerer 1972, pp.66-70)

Surprisingly, though, early IQ research played almost no role in the exclusionary legislation of the 1920s. As Herrnstein and Snyderman 1983, pp.993 explain:

> Of the total committee hearings and addenda for both House or Senate, then, allegations of innate intellectual inferiority of immigrants represented a minute fraction... The report teems with reasons for keeping "inferior" immigrants out of the country, but it contains no mention whatever of intelligence or intelligence testing. No mention,

WHOA, WHOA, WHOA. YOU CAN BE CHINESE, BUT NOT *CHINESE* CHINESE.

either, in the Minority Report, written by Representatives Adolph Sabath and Samuel Dickstein who label the proposed act as racist and discriminatory, and who uphold the worth of the immigrant. Even when the innate characteristics of immigrants were the central issue, as in both of these reports, neither intelligence nor testing came up.

If intelligence testing was of little importance in committee hearings, it played an even smaller role in floor debate. In both chambers of Congress, concern focused on two topics: the influx of cheap labor via immigration and the general, though unspecified, inferiority of immigrants.

For a detailed table of the annual quotas effective in 1929, see Ngai 1999, p.74. Note that east Asian *countries* were given quotas, albeit tiny ones. Yet even these slots were closed to Asian *individuals*: "China, Japan, India, and Siam each received the minimum quota of one hundred, but the law excluded the native citizens of those countries from immigration because they were deemed to be racially ineligible to citizenship. Thus Congress created the oddity of immigration quotas for non-Chinese persons from China, non-Japanese persons from Japan, non-Indian persons from India, and so on." (Ngai 1999, pp.72-3)

p.25. Prominent works criticizing the effects of immigration include Borjas 2001, 2014, 2016, Salam 2018, Krikorian 2008, 2010, Coulter 2015a, and Brimelow 1995. While many interpret Jones 2016 as highly critical of low-skilled immigration, the actual text is strikingly *pro*-immigration:

WHAT? NORDICS ARE SUPERIOR.

WHY IS THIS SUDDENLY CONTROVERSIAL?

About a decade ago, dozens of American economists signed an open letter in support of more immigration. The letter touched on many points: that less-skilled immigrants appear to push down the wages of U.S.-born citizens little if at all, that immigration helps rich-country economies in ways that don't show up in official statistics, and that the biggest beneficiaries of less-skilled immigration are the immigrants themselves... I've always been glad I signed this letter: it sums up the great promise of immigration... For people who care about ending the deepest poverty, migration should be at the top of the list of potential cures. (Jones 2016, pp.160-1)

CHAPTER 2:
TRILLION-DOLLAR BILLS ON THE SIDEWALK

pp.28–29. See Caplan 2013b for the original statement of this thought experiment.

p.30. The world's leading introductory economics textbook includes "A country's standard of living depends on its ability to produce goods and services" on its list of the top ten principles of economics. (Mankiw 2015, p.13; for elaboration, see pp.523–46) Competing textbooks, regardless of the authors' ideology, make the very same point: See e.g. Cowen and Tabarrok 2018, pp.529–51, and Krugman and Wells 2017, pp.407–48.

p.31, panel 3.   Leading impediments to wealth creation include bad economic policies (Sachs and Warner 1995a, 1995b; Gwartney et al. 2017, pp.1–26), poor management (Bloom and van Reenen 2010), war (Collier 1999; Blattman and Miguel 2010), geography (Gallup et al. 1999; Sachs 2003), and corruption (Drury et al. 2006; Mo 2001).

pp.32–33.   This discussion draws heavily on Clemens et al. forthcoming. While estimates of the gains of migration vary, all leading papers find enormous effects. See Hendricks 2002, Iregui 2005, Bertoli et al. 2008, Clemens and Pritchett 2008, McKenzie et al. 2010, and Abramitzky et al. 2012.

pp.34–35.   This discussion draws heavily on Clemens 2011. As usual, estimates of the effect of open borders on Gross World Product vary, but are consistently enormous. See Hamilton and Whalley 1984, Moses and Letnes 2004, 2005, Klein and Ventura 2009, Kennan 2013, and Delogu et al. 2018. Clemens and Pritchett 2016 grant that given pessimistic assumptions, full open borders is no longer economically optimal; the benefits of drastic liberalization, however, remain massive.

Borjas 2014, pp.167-8, offers the only serious quantitative challenge to these eye-popping figures, arguing that they are grossly overstated because they ignore migrants' emotional attachment to their birthplaces. Caplan 2014a shows, however, that Borjas entertains absurdly high monetary values for these attachments. Why absurd? Borjas looks at how many dollars you would have to pay the *average American* to relocate, then imputes similar figures to even the world's poorest and most eager migrants. All the benefits of open borders go away if you "only" assume that Haitian immigrants pay a $140,000 emotional cost to leave Port-au-Prince! Borjas 2015, p.971 repeats his original argument but pleads agnosticism on the numbers: "Of course, we have no idea what the costs of migration will actually be if migration restrictions were to be removed and billions of people from poor countries were on the move." But agnosticism is not warranted; while people around the world feel *some* emotional attachment to their homeland, the monetary value of these attachments is clearly tiny compared to the gains of migration. See Clemens and Pritchett 2016, pp.11–16 for a more extended response to the Borjas challenge.

p.36, panel 4.   Researchers find large, positive effects of immigration on housing prices; when immigrants increase regional population by 1%, housing prices rise by roughly 1%. See especially Saiz 2007, as well as Ottaviano and Peri 2006 and Gonzalez and Ortega 2013. Since roughly two-thirds of Americans own their own home, these gains would be widely dispersed. There is, however, some evidence that immigration (especially low-skilled immigration) lowers *local* housing prices by encouraging the exit of wealthier natives. (Saiz and Wachter 2011, Sá 2015) In other words, immigration enriches the *average* homeowner, but some lose nonetheless.

p.36, panel 5.   Roughly 25% of direct-care workers are foreign-born (Espinoza 2017), well above the foreign-born share of the workforce.

p.36, panel 6. See especially Cortés and Tessada 2011.

p.36, panel 7. Rising home prices standardly lead to large increases in construction, except in regions with strict land-use regulation. For an overview, see Glaeser 2017.

p.38, panel 1. Even economists who emphasize the negative effects of immigration on native wages report small—and mixed—effects. Borjas and Katz 2007, p.49, estimate that, in the long run, extra Mexican migration from 1980–2000 reduced U.S. native dropouts' wages by a grand total of 4.8%, and college graduates' wages by 0.5%. They also conclude, however, that Mexican immigration *increased* the wages of native high school graduates by 1.2% and those with some college by 0.7%.

p.38, panel 2. Immigration increases labor demand through two channels—one obvious, the other subtle. The obvious: More immigrants means more potential customers. The subtle: Since migration increases foreigners' productivity, they have more resources to offer in the marketplace. As a rule, sellers profit from more and richer customers.

   Aside: It is equally correct to say that "Immigrants who *sell* what you *buy* help you by increasing labor demand." All else equal, your real wage—the amount of stuff an hour of your labor actually buys—rises whenever the supply of *anything* you consume becomes more abundant. If a new immigrant restaurant opens in my neighborhood, for example, I effectively receive a raise, because my salary now permits me to buy a slightly better basket of goods.

p.38, panel 3. How can native workers possibly profit when labor supply rises? Through specialization and trade. When the supply of low-skilled workers goes up, so does the demand for higher-skilled workers to manage them. When non-English-speaking immigrants increase the supply of cooks and dishwashers, this increases the demand for English-speaking waiters. See Peri and Sparber 2009 and D'Amuri and Peri 2014 for a careful analysis of this mechanism, and Ottaviano and Peri 2012 for further evidence.

p.39, panel 2. By 2005–8, roughly 20% of tenure-track faculty at four-year U.S. universities were foreign-born, with the share rising to 33% in the physical sciences and 43% in engineering/computer science. (Kim et al. 2012, pp.28–9)

pp.40–41. The Arithmetic Fallacy is roughly what statisticians call "Simpson's Paradox." See Wagner 1982 and Kievit et al. 2013 for readable introductions, and Caplan 2005, 2010 for the immigration connection.

pp.41, panel 3. Why do both groups' incomes rise under open borders? As usual, because migrants' productivity drastically rises—and native consumers share the bounty. The precise figures, to be clear, are merely illustrative, and assume that under open borders, the population ends up half native, half foreign. So, even though average native income rises to $60,000 and average foreign income rises to $20,000, the receiving country's overall average income *falls* to $40,000.

p.42, panels 2–3. World Bank 2014 estimates of Chinese and Indian GDP in 2014 U.S. dollars, with 1976 figures adjusted for U.S. GDP deflator. (World Bank 2018a, 2018b, 2018c)

p.42, panel 4. Useful analyses of Chinese and Indian economic liberalization and development include Sachs and Woo 2001, and Kotwal et al. 2011.

p.42, panel 5-6.   See Woetzel et al. 2009, esp. pp.55-65 and Sankhe 2010, esp. pp.37–51 on internal migration and urbanization in China and India.

p.43.   For further discussion, see Caplan and Naik 2015, pp.185-190.

p.44.   For more, see Caplan and Naik 2015, pp.190-1.

p.46.   For an excellent introduction to diaspora dynamics, see Collier 2013, pps.37-53, 166-8. Caplan 2014b argues that, contrary to Collier, diaspora dynamics bolster the case for open borders.

p.47, panels 1–2.   For the complete ruling in the González case, see FindLaw 2018.

p.47, panels 3–5.   For historical context and data on Puerto Rican migration, see Whalen 2005, esp. pps.2, 11. Caplan 2014c argues that Puerto Rico provides a compelling illustration of diaspora dynamics under open borders.

p.47, panel 6.   The current population of Puerto Rico is roughly 3.3 million. (Wikipedia 2018a) According to Whalen 2005, p.11, 3.4 million people of Puerto Rican descent were already living in the United States in 2000.

p.48, panels 1–2.   Wikipedia 2018b.

p.48, panels 3–4.   Ratha et al. 2016.

p.48, panel 5.   See Gibson and McKenzie 2011 for a review of research on brain drain.

pp.49–50.   This discussion draws heavily on Pritchett 2006, pp.43–62, and Pritchett et al. 2006, as well as Clemens and Pritchett 2008.

p.49, panel 4.   Pritchett et al. 2006, pp.29–30.

CHAPTER 3:
THE NATIVE'S BURDEN?

p.56, panel 8.   According to Snopes 2018, Sutton claims he never actually spoke these words, although he did write a book alluding to the quote.

p.57, panel 5.   Friedman 1999. For context, see Caplan 2008.

p.58, panels 2–5.   See Cowen and Tabarrok 2018, pp.368–371.

p.59, panel 1.   In 2015, combined local, state, and federal spending came to $601.7 billion for means-tested medical care and $447.8 billion for other means-tested spending, bringing total means-tested spending to $1.05 trillion. (USGovernmentSpending 2018)

p.59, panel 2.   In 2015, the U.S. government spent $887.8 billion on Social Security and $546.2 billion on Medicare, summing to $1.434 trillion. (Office of Management and Budget 2017, pp.83) Combined local, state, and federal education spending in the same year comes to $1.03 trillion. (USGovernmentSpending 2018)

p.60.   Migration Policy Institute 2016. Note that this webpage is updated annually.

p.61, panel 1.   In the most recent statistics (2013-4), average U.S. K–12 spending in 2015–16 dollars was $12,000 per pupil in average daily attendance and $11,226 per pupil in fall enrollment. (Snyder et al. 2018, p.382) p.62.   For an introduction to the demographics of retirement systems, see Schwarz and Arias 2014, esp. pps.1–11, 41–56.

p.64, panel 1.   Blau and Mackie 2016.

p.64, panels 2–5.   For background, see Blau and Mackie 2016, pp.247–75.

pp.66-8.   For an introduction to Net Present Value (also called "Present Discounted Value" or simply "Present Value"), see Mishkin 2016, pp.110–13.

p.69, panel 2.   Blau and Mackie 2016, p.343, "All Immigrants" figures. Disclosure: This section of Blau and Mackie estimates immigrants' fiscal effects in *six* different scenarios.

Scenario #	Forecasting Assumption	Public Goods Assumption
1	CBO Long-term Budget Outlook	Congestible Only
2	CBO Long-term Budget Outlook	With Non-Interest Public Goods
3	CBO Long-term Budget Outlook with Deficit Reduction	Congestible Only
4	CBO Long-term Budget Outlook with Deficit Reduction	With Non-Interest Public Goods
5	No Budget Adjustments	Congestible Only
6	No Budget Adjustments	With Non-Interest Public Goods

Why do I report figures for Scenario #1, when most of the other scenarios are less optimistic?

First, the No Budget Adjustments Assumption, which ignores even readily foreseeable information about future U.S. finances, is clearly the worst forecasting assumption of the bunch. (Blau and Mackie 2016, p.323) Both CBO Long-term Budget Outlook assumptions are superior because they account for foreseeable social and economic changes, such as aging. In this panel, I conservatively rely on the *more* pessimistic of the two CBO scenarios.

Second, the "Congestible Only" assumption is better because it tries to distinguish between rival and non-rival goods. ("Congestible" is a synonym for "rival.") The alternate assumption absurdly treats all spending as fully rival.

p.69, panel 3.   Blau and Mackie 2016, p.343, "All Immigrants" figures. The disclosure in the previous note applies here as well.

p.69, panel 5.   Blau and Mackie 2016, p.343. These figures come from Scenario #3, as explained in the note for p.69, panel 2. All things considered, the figures in this panel are not only the most optimistic; they are also the most credible. The CBO Long-term Budget Outlook accounts for future social and economic changes, but treats existing government policies as immutable. (Blau and Mackie 2016, p.323) Given large recent and expected budget deficits, however, spending cuts and tax increases are both highly likely in the medium term. (Congressional Budget Office 2018) The CBO Long-term Budget Outlook with Deficit Reduction accordingly assumes that the government *slowly* moves in this direction, gradually raising taxes by 3% and cutting spending by 3% by 2035. (Blau and Mackie 2016, p.323)

p.72, panels 1–2.   Blau and Mackie 2016, p.341, "HS" and "<HS" rows, "Average Total Impact" column.

Since we are now considering the fiscal effects of *additional* immigrants, I here use the "Averages Based on Recent Immigrants," Scenario #1. Note: "No public goods included in benefits" is equivalent to the "congestible only" assumption that appears in Blau and Mackie 2016, p.343.

p.73, panels 2–3.   Blau and Mackie 2016, p.341, "HS" and "<HS" rows, "0–24" column.

p.73, panels 5–6.   Blau and Mackie 2016, p.341, "HS" and "<HS" rows, "65+" column.

p.75, panel 2.   Friedman 1999.

p.76, panel 1.   "When a marginal cost allocation of public goods is assumed, instead of the average cost allocation, the total net fiscal impact of the first generation group becomes much lower than that of the two native-born groups." (Blau and Mackie 2016, p.320; for details, see Scenarios #1 and #2 on p.312)

pp.76–7.   See Tabarrok 2000 for exploration of the parallels between immigration and fertility.

p.78, panel 2.   I was once accused of "suicidal compassion" for immigrants; see Caplan 2013c for my response.

p.79, panels 1–2.   See Caplan 2007, pp.36–9 on "antiforeign bias," humans' tendency to underestimate the economic benefits of interacting with foreigners.

CHAPTER 4:
CRIMES AGAINST CULTURE

p.84, panel 2.   Voltaire 1980, p.41.

p.85, panels 1–4.   This section is partly inspired by my debate with Stephen Balch. (Institute for the Study of Western Civilization 2014) For follow-up discussion, see Caplan 2014d, 2014e.

p.86, panel 1.   For a general history of probability and risk analysis, with extensive discussion of Gauss's contributions, see Bernstein 1998. Of course, most non-Western civilizations have used numbers to inform decision making. But the idea of *quantifying uncertainty* remained in its infancy until mathematicians Fermat and Pascal launched probability theory during the European Renaissance. (Bernstein 1998, pp.2–6)

p.86, panel 2.   For the probability of being struck by lightning, see National Weather Service 2018.

p.87, panel 4.   Nowrasteh 2016, p.6 reports 3,432 total U.S. deaths from terrorism during this period, 3,024 of whom were killed by foreign-born terrorists.

p.88, panel 4.   FBI statistics exclude the 2,983 deaths from the 9/11 attacks. When you add these deaths to official FBI statistics (Disaster Center 2017), the sum is approximately 772,000 total murders.

p.88, panel 5.   The total U.S. death rate during this period peaked at 8.9 per 1,000. (Knoema 2018) The murder rate during this period peaked in 1980 at 1 in 9,781. (Disaster Center 2017) p.88, panel 6. Nowrasteh 2016, pp.4–5 reports a 1-in-3.6 million risk of death from foreign-born domestic terrorism. Dividing by .88 yields a 1-in-3.2 million risk of death from all terrorism.

p.89, panel 1. This meme was first posted by Donald Trump Jr. on his Twitter account. (Hauser 2016)

p.89, panel 5. In Plato's account of Socrates's deathbed oration, the philosopher famously counsels, "[T]he unexamined life is not worth living..." (Plato 2002, p.41)

p.90, panel 3. Nowrasteh 2016, p.8 calculates that "one foreign-born terrorist entered the United States for every 7.38 million non-terrorist foreigners," implying that 99.999986% were *not* terrorists.

p.91, panel 2. See especially the National Academy of Sciences review (Waters and Pineau 2015, pp.326–330) as well as Lee and Martinez 2009 and Nowrasteh 2015. Even researchers at the Center for Immigration Studies claim not that immigrants are crime-prone, but that the evidence is "confused due to a lack of good data and contrary information." (Camarota and Vaughan 2009, p.1)

p.91, panel 3. United States Census Bureau 2018b. To reproduce my figures for the native population, divide each year's number of natives in Adult Correctional Facilities by the native population. Similarly, the foreign-born rate equals the number of foreign-born in these facilities divided by the foreign-born population.

p.92, panel 1. United States Census Bureau 2018b. To reproduce my figures for naturalized citizens, divide each year's number of incarcerated naturalized citizens by the number of naturalized citizens.

p.92, panel 2. United States Census Bureau 2018b. To reproduce my figures for non-citizens, divide each year's number of incarcerated non-citizens by the number of non-citizens. Note: If illegal immigration exceeds conventional estimates, then as a matter of arithmetic, conventional estimates *overstate* the criminality of non-citizens.

p.92, panel 3. Carson 2018, p.13 reports that over 21% of federal inmates were noncitizens, roughly triple their share of the U.S. population. In 2016, 13,300 federal inmates were serving time for immigration offenses. (Carson, p.19) Roughly 80% of immigration offenses are for illegal reentry. (United States Sentencing Commission 2017)

p.93, panel 3. Waters and Pineau 2015, p.327. For further discussion, see Waters and Pineau 2015, pp.330–2 as well as Lee and Martinez 2009 and Nowrasteh 2015.

p.93, panel 4. See Waters and Pineau 2015, p.329: "Although the second generation has higher crime rates than the first generation, their rates are generally lower than or very similar to the crime rate of the native-born in general."

p.95, panel 1. Psychologists have a name—"availability bias"—for humans' tendency to inflate the likelihood of vivid events. See Kahneman 2011, pp.129–145 for a review of the evidence, and

Kuran and Sunstein 1999 for analysis of the dysfunctional political effects of this bias.

p.96, panel 1. Ryan 2013, p.7. Language data are only available for persons five years and older. For obvious reasons, the Census does not ask about the speaking ability of infants or toddlers.

p.96, panel 2. Ryan 2013, p.11.

p.96, panel 3. I count speakers as "fluent" if they (a) speak only English at home, or (b) claim to speak English "very well." In 2010, 91% of the population so qualified. (Ryan 2013, p.3) In 1980, 95% so qualified. (Bureau of the Census 1984, p.1–12)

p.97, panel 3. Census-takers classified a majority of late 19th-century arrivals as simply unable to speak English. Their English improved over time, but since the Census used a binary measure ("Speaks English" or "Does Not Speak English") we can safely assume that most never became fluent. (Vigdor 2015, pp.81–84) Stevens 1999, p.555 confirms the common-sense conclusion that, "[P]roficiency in a second language among adults is strongly related to age at immigration."

p.97, panel 4. Chua 2011, p.86.

p.97, panel 5. Stevens 1999, pp.569–71, for example, estimates that nearly 100% of immigrants who arrive in infancy and remain in the country attain full fluency. Adult arrivals are far less likely to do so, even after decades of residence. See also Stevens 2015.

p.98, panels 2–3. Alba 2004, p.7.

p.99, panels 3–5. Rumbaut et al. 2006, pp.456–8.

p.100, panel 3. This point is heavily inspired by Smith 2012:

> [G]lobalization has half-Americanized half the world already. 19th-Century immigrants may have been *racially* more similar to America's white native majority, but they were less familiar with democracy, with the English language, with America via movies and music and TV, with American-style market capitalism, with Coke and McDonald's and Microsoft and Google and many other American firms, with blue jeans and free speech and religious tolerance, than a 19th-century immigrant from the Habsburg Empire or tsarist Russia.

p.100, panel 4. Wikipedia 2018c.

p.100, panel 5. Wikipedia 2018d.

p.101, panel 1. For overviews on the social benefits of trust, see Algan and Cahuc 2014 and Nannestad 2008.

p.101, panel 2. Map from Ortiz-Ospina and Roser 2017.

Putnam 2007 famously argues that immigration undermines trust by increasing ethnic diversity. But even in Putnam's own analysis (pp.151–3), this is a relatively minor effect; diverse American communities have low trust almost entirely because blacks and Hispanics have low trust, not because they are ethnically mixed. (Caplan 2017a) The far stronger reason to expect low-skilled immigration to reduce trust is the well-documented fact that trust in the third world is low. (Algan and Cahuc 2014, pp.62–4; Ortiz-Ospina and Roser 2017)

p.102, panel 1. Pieces arguing that trust assimilation is low include Algan and Cahuc 2010 and Uslaner 2008.

p.102, panels 2–3. Studies finding high assimilation include Dinesen 2012, and Dinesen and Hooghe 2010. Caplan 2017a notes that Uslaner 2008 finds only small effects and relies almost entirely on descendants of European immigrants. Algan and Cahuc 2010's modestly broader sample finds just 45% trust persistence.

p.102, panel 4. Caplan 2017a. Throughout this book, I try to rely on an overall topic-by-topic review of the research rather than presenting original results. But to the best of my knowledge, no trust specialist has taken full advantage of U.S. data to estimate trust persistence, so I had to fill this role myself.

Disclosure: The qualification "descendants of willing immigrants" is crucial. "Descendants" is crucial because first-generation trust *is* highly persistent. I estimate 70% persistence for immigrants, versus just 28% for their descendants. "Willing immigrants" is crucial because (a) almost all African Americans are descended from slaves, (b) African Americans are a numerous group, and (c) both African Americans and Africans generally have very low trust. If you count Africans like other immigrants, estimated trust persistence for immigrants' descendants doubles to 56%. Why distinguish between the descendants of free versus forced migrants? Because slavery persistently damaged trust in Africa (Nunn and Wantchekon 2011), and it seems plausible to think it had a similar effect in the United States.

p.103, panel 1. For skeptical analyses of the social benefits of trust, see Berggren et al. 2008 and Roth 2009. Bjørnskov 2007 finds that few alleged cross-country predictors of trust are genuinely significant; even the much-studied effect of ethnic diversity is marginal. Nannestad 2008 also presents detailed evidence that, popularizers notwithstanding, the social benefits of trust remain questionable.

p.103, panel 2. Putnam 2007, pp.144–50.

p.103, panel 3. Roth 2009, p.117.

p.103, panel 4. Butler et al. 2016, p.1165–7.

p.103, panel 5. On the distinction between trust and trustworthiness, see Glaeser et al. 2000.

p.104, panel 3. Schoenberg 1950, p.39.

pp.106–7. See generally Caplan 2014d, 2014e.

p.107, panel 3. The true author of this quote is unknown. (Quote Investigator 2015)

CHAPTER 5:
THE GOLDEN GOOSE ON TRIAL

p.112. Economists call this the problem of "political externalities of immigration." See Naik 2018a for an overview of the argument, including numerous links to defenders and critics.

p.113, panel 4. Caplan 2007.

p.114, panels 3–5.	All figures are from my analysis of the General Social Survey, 1980–2012, using two-party vote shares. Variable identifiers: pres80-pres12, if80who-if2012who. By "white" I mean "non-Hispanic white."
p.115, panel 1.	Contrary to popular opinion, the effect of material self-interest on voting and public opinion is slight. The primary drivers of political behavior are ideology and identity, not dollars and cents. See e.g. Mansbridge 1990 and Caplan 2007, pp.148–51.
p.115, panel 2.	Wikipedia 2018e.
p.115, panel 3.	In 2015, 90% of Indian households with children contained two married adults, versus 73% for the U.S. as a whole. (Pew Research Center 2017; Bureau of the Census 2018)
p.115, panel 4.	Junn et al. 2011, p.527.
p.115, panel 6.	While political scientists have long debated government responsiveness to public opinion, almost all acknowledge a major connection. The best single work on this title probably remains Gilens 2012, especially pp.50–123, which analyzes a large data set of policy-relevant surveys and actual political results. This approach likely understates the power of public opinion, because pollsters rarely bother to ask about extremely popular or unpopular proposals.
p.116, panel 1.	Nowrasteh and Wilson 2017 provides a detailed comparison of the political views of immigrants versus natives. I have reanalyzed the same data set (the General Social Survey, 2000–16) to simplify the presentation, but our overall results are quite consistent.
p.116, panel 2.	GSS variable identifier POLVIEWS.
p.116, panel 3.	GSS variable identifier HELPNOT.
p.116, panel 4.	GSS variable identifiers TAXPOOR, TAXMID, and TAXRICH.
p.117, panel 1.	GSS variable identifier NATFARE. All results on this page analyze opinion for 2000–16.
p.117, panel 2.	GSS variable identifiers NATSOC, NATHEAL, NATEDUC, NATENVIR, and NATARMS.
p.117, panels 4–7.	GSS variables identifiers ABANY, MARHOMO, GRASS, and SPKMSLM. Since social attitudes have rapidly liberalized as the foreign-born population share has risen, some of these patterns are not instantly visible in the data; to detect them, you must look year-by-year. In technical terms, a multiple regression of these social attitudes on nativity and year consistently confirms that the foreign-born are more socially conservative on all four questions.
p.117, panels 8–9.	GSS variable identifier LETIN1. Remember that this averages attitudes from 2000 to 2016, so there is no real conflict with recent Gallup data showing markedly higher support for liberalization. (Brenan 2018)
p.118, panels 3–4.	See Caplan and Naik 2015, pp.193–5 for the construction of these measures. The "U.S. Mean" is the average answer for *all* respondents in the U.S.-based General Social Survey, which includes natives, immigrants, and foreign citizens. The normal distributions are a simplification; the critical facts are (a) the mean and (b) subgroups' deviation from the mean (measured in standard deviations).
p.119, panel 2.	GSS variable identifier VOTE12.
p.119, panel 3.	GSS variable identifier VOTE12, sub-sample with DEGREE=0.
p.119, panels 4–5.	On low influence of poor voters, see Gilens 2012. Critics accuse Gilens of under-

stating government responsiveness to *middle*-class voters. (Bashir 2015, Matthews 2016) But even the authors of the two main critical pieces do not dispute Gilens's conclusion that poor voters lack political influence. (Private email correspondence with both Bashir and Matthews)

p.119, panel 6. See e.g. Nowrasteh and Wilson 2017.

p.120, panel 2. Gochenour and Nowrasteh 2014, pp.5–8, surveys this literature; leading papers include Alesina et al. 2001, Alesina et al. 2018, and Soroka et al. 2006.

p.120, panel 3. Bay and Pedersen 2006, pps.424–8. The table on p.428 seems to indicate 68% initial support, but only because it excludes the undecided respondents shown on p.425. Since "Change Position" includes a change to "undecided" (p.434, fn 9), I base the treatment effect on the authors' statement (p.428) that, "Only 45 percent of the entire sample are ready to support a basic income scheme that they have been reminded will include non-citizens."

p.121, panels 1–2. See e.g. Derbyshire 2015.

p.123. Top papers on the long-run effects of national ancestry include Putterman and Weil 2010, Comin et al. 2010, and Spolaore and Wacziarg 2013. "Advanced" by what standard? The researchers' three main measures are: (a) when your ancestors adopted agriculture, (b) when your ancestors developed centralized governments (usually called "state history"), and (c) when your ancestors adopted specific critical technologies. For detailed critiques of all three papers, see Caplan 2016a, 2016b, and 2016c.

p.124. The original researchers barely hint at the implications for immigration, but my colleague Garett Jones explicitly bases his case for immigration restrictions on their work. (Jones 2015) The "SAT Score" in the title of his talk refers to ancestral "state history" (S), "agriculture" (A), and "technology" (T), not the familiar college admissions test.

p.125, panels 1–4. Caplan 2016d highlights that China, India, and the U.S. are all serious outliers for Putterman and Weil 2010.

p.125, panel 5. Caplan 2016e shows that population-weighting vitiates Putterman and Weil's 2010 results for both agriculture and state history. To the best of my knowledge, no one has reestimated Comin et al. 2010's results for ancestral technologies using population weighting.

p.126, panels 1–3. See Caplan 2016a, 2016b, 2016c, and 2017b. Unlike ancestry results, the geographic results are robust to population weighting. (Caplan 2016e)

p.126, panel 4. In fact, Putterman and Weil's 2010 results imply that moving the world's population to the United States would increase world GDP to almost four times its current level! (Caplan 2016d)

p.127, panels 2–4. The research literature on cognitive ability is vast. For an overview, see Jensen 1998, esp. pp.270–305. Despite public controversy, there is a strong research consensus on the basic science of intelligence. (Gottfredsen 1994)

p.128, panel 1. This map (IQ Research 2018) is derived from Lynn and Vanhanen 2002; Rindermann et al. 2009 and Lynn and Meisenberg 2010 present quite similar estimates. Wicherts et al. 2010 argues that earlier researchers seriously underestimate sub-Saharan African IQ, but still concludes that the region is well below the world average.

p.128, panel 2.   IQ is not only strongly correlated with national income (Jones 2016; Lynn and Vanhanen 2002); when "raced" against other explanatory variables, it outperforms almost all of them. (Jones and Schneider 2006)

p.128, panels 3–4.   Rich countries have less serious crime and more democracy than poor countries. (van Zanden et al. 2014, pps.154–5, 173–4) Given the positive correlation between GDP and IQ, we can infer that high-IQ countries have less serious crime and more democracy than low-IQ countries. Rindermann et al. 2009 documents the correlation between national IQ and both crime and democracy. Note: Even if income, not IQ, statistically accounted for these patterns, IQ would still ultimately deserve some credit as long as IQ genuinely caused higher income.

p.129, panels 1–2.   Jones 2016.

p.129, panel 3.   See Jones 2016, pp.85–102.

p.129, panels 4–5.   Jones 2016, pp.1–14; Jones and Schneider 2008.

p.130, panel 1.   Jones 2016, pp.103–37; Caplan 2007.

p.130, panel 2.   Caplan and Miller 2010.

p.130, panel 3.   Jones 2016, pp.161–3; Coulter 2015a. To the best of my knowledge, Jones never publicly praised Coulter, but Coulter has strongly praised Jones. Her Facebook page links to the book, stating, "Which reminds me: Low IQ immigrants are lowering your income, your freedom, your way of life. Read this book." (Coulter 2015b) While *Hive Mind*'s actual discussion of immigration is rather positive (Jones 2016, pp.153–63), he has subsequently drawn far more negative implications. (Jones 2017)

p.131, panel 1.   Both of *Hive Mind*'s measures of U.S. IQ put it at 98. (Jones 2016, p.170) Estimates of *humanity's* average IQ (as opposed to *nations'* average IQs) are scarce, but Rindermann 2018, p.448 estimates population-weighted global IQ at 87.

p.131, panels 2–3.   All GDP figures are adjusted for Purchasing Power Parity (PPP). (World Bank 2018e) I use 2016 data because this is the most recent year where World GDP is available.

To follow the calculations, note that in *Hive Mind*, Jones builds upon his earlier work with Schneider, which estimates that raising national IQ by 1 point raises the natural logarithm of per-capita GDP by .061—approximately 6.1%. (Jones 2016, p.11; Jones and Schneider 2006, p.90) This implies that an 11-point fall in IQ multiplies initial GDP by exp(-.061*11)=0.51. If we drop the PPP adjustment, World GDP is only $10,201, implying that open borders would raise World GDP by 188%! (World Bank 2018e)

p.132.   Jones 2016, pp.49–64.

p.133, panel 1.   For overviews of the developmental effects of international adoption, see Juffer and van IJzendoorn 2009, and van IJzendoorn et al. 2005.

p.133, panel 2.   The key Swedish studies are Dalen et al. 2008 and Odenstad et al. 2008.

p.133, panels 3–4.   For a survey of the physical benefits of international adoption, see van IJzendoorn et al. 2007 and Juffer et al. 2009, pp.175–7.

p.133, panels 5–6. For a survey of the cognitive benefits of international adoption, see van IJzendoorn 2005 and Juffer et al. 2009, pps.178–180.

p.134, panels 1–2. For overviews of the relevant research on the weak effect of family environment on intelligence and the fade-out of early nurture effects, see Caplan 2011, pps.49–51, 76–80. See also Caplan 2016e.

p.134, panel 3. Dalen et al. 2008 and Odenstad et al. 2008 confirm large effects of international adoption on adult IQ; Vinnerljung et al. 2010 finds comparable effects of international adoption on high school performance. This research has a slightly pessimistic tone because it focuses on the fact that international adoptees score worse than native-born Swedes. They do, but international adoptees also do better than they would have done *if they had remained in their countries of birth.* (Caplan 2017c, 2017d) Note: The latter comparisons make the conservative assumption that adoptees would have grown up to have average IQ and educational performance for their home countries. Since adoptees tend to come from disadvantaged backgrounds (including third-world orphanages), they probably would have been well *below* average if they had stayed behind, implying even larger cognitive gains of adoption.

p.135, panel 2. For general discussions of nurture effects, see Caplan 2011, pp.37–91, Segal 2000, and Harris 2009.

p.137. For a history of the Berlin Wall, see Taylor 2008.

CHAPTER 6:
KEYHOLE SOLUTIONS

p.140, panel 3. See Johns Hopkins Medicine 2018 for an introduction.

p.141, panel 1. To the best of my (and his) knowledge, Tim Harford originated the phrase "keyhole solution" in *The Undercover Economist*. (Harford 2012, pp.138–143) He has also done much to popularize the concept.

p.143. See Naik 2018b for overview and references, and Caplan 2012b for discussion of economic, fiscal, cultural, and political keyhole solutions.

p.144. Nathaniel Smith labels this the DRITI approach (short for "Don't Restrict Immigration; Tax It"). See Smith 2010, pp.109–124 for a policy blueprint.

p.147, panel 5. Nowrasteh and Cole 2013.

p.148. See Nowrasteh and Cole 2013 for further discussion.

p.151, panel 1. Though Trump has not strictly fulfilled his campaign promise "for a total and complete shutdown of Muslims entering the United States until our country's representatives can figure out what the hell is going on" (Johnson 2015), legal immigration from Muslim-majority countries has dramatically fallen during his administration. (Bier 2018)

p.151, panels 2–4. Comparative politics specialists continue to debate *why* the Muslim world has such a grim human rights record, but the fact is well established. See e.g. Fish 2002, Stepan and Robertson 2003, and Donno and Russett 2004.

p.151, panel 2.	In 2014, 276 Nigerian schoolgirls in the town of Chibok were kidnapped and forced into sexual slavery by the Islamist terrorist organization Boko Haram. Some were murdered, and over 100 are still missing. (Habila 2016)
p.152.	See generally Caplan 2015a.
p.152, panel 3.	Wikipedia 2018f.
p.154, panel 4.	Political scientists have long known that average citizens are politically apathetic (see e.g. Schubert, Dye, and Zeigler 2015) and participation among the eligible foreign-born is especially low in a wide range of countries. (Diehl and Wüst 2010) Globally, heavy migration to *both* Western democracies and oil-rich Gulf monarchies makes it clear that prosperity, not democracy, is the primary draw.
p.155, panel 3.	Some colleges even charge out-of-state tuition plus an extra foreign student surcharge! (Redden 2015)
p.156, panel 2.	See Office of the Assistant Secretary for Planning and Evaluation 2009 for the gory details.
p.156, panel 3.	USA.gov 2018 provides full instructions.
p.157, panel 1.	For the Bracero quotes, see National Museum of American History 2018a.
p.157, panels 2–3.	For details on the H1-B, H2-A, and H2-B temporary work programs, see USCIS 2017, USCIS 2018a, and USCIS 2018b.
p.160.	All Bible quotes from Genesis 18:20–32 of the New International Version. (Bible Gateway 2011a) In the original Bible story, Sodom lacks even ten righteous men, so God destroys the city anyway.

CHAPTER 7:
ALL ROADS LEAD TO OPEN BORDERS

p.166.	For a more detailed discussion, see Caplan and Naik 2015, pp.195–200.
pp.167–170.	Carens 1987 famously defends open borders from utilitarian, Rawlsian, and Nozickian premises.
p.170.	See Caplan 2013d for elaboration.
p.171.	Posner prefers the label "wealth maximization," but the substance is identical. See especially Posner 1979, 1980. In his later writings, Posner seems to largely abandon cost-benefit analysis in favor of a "pragmatism" that eschews almost any radical reform; see for example Posner 2003.
p.172.	Though Lee is primarily known as a politician, his writings are unusually philosophical for a man of action. The closing words of his history of modern Singapore: "[W]e stand a better chance of not failing if we abide by the basic principles that have helped us progress: social cohesion through sharing the benefits of progress, equal opportunities for all, and meritocracy, with the best man or woman for the job, especially as leaders in government." (Lee 2000)
p.174.	All Bible quotes from Luke 10:30-37 of the New International Version. (Bible Gateway 2011b)

pp.175–176. Kant's classic statement:

> Juridical punishment can never be administered merely as a means for promoting another good, either with regard to the criminal himself or to civil society, but must in all cases be imposed only because the individual on whom it is inflicted has committed a crime. For one man ought never to be dealt with merely as a means subservient to the purpose of another, nor be mixed up with the subjects of real right... He must first be found guilty and punishable, before there can be any thought of drawing from his punishment any benefit for himself or his fellow-citizens. (Kant 1887, p.195)

pp.177–180. Besides Huemer 2010, see also his critiques of social contract theory and democratic legitimacy in Huemer 2013, pp.20–80. Caplan 2012c analyzes the "trespassing" objection to open borders.

p.181, panel 2. High-quality surveys actually find that even Republicans are *slowly* becoming less hostile to immigration. (Brenan 2018) But 35% of Republicans now name immigration as "the nation's top problem," an all-time high (Newport 2018b), and Republican politicians and pundits are plainly more opposed.

p.183, panel 1. Reagan 1987. Reagan's Farewell Address almost explicitly calls for open borders:

> I've spoken of the shining city all my political life, but I don't know if I ever quite communicated what I saw when I said it. But in my mind it was a tall, proud city built on rocks stronger than oceans, windswept, God-blessed, and teeming with people of all kinds living in harmony and peace; a city with free ports that hummed with commerce and creativity. And if there had to be city walls, the walls had doors and the doors were open to anyone with the will and the heart to get here. (Reagan 1989; see also Caplan 2017e)

p.184, panel 4. This sign is not an expression of post–Pearl Harbor hysteria. It dates from soon after World War I, where the U.S. and Japan both fought for the Allies. (National Museum of American History 2018b)

pp.185–6. Trump 2016.

p.187. This is the classic economic case for free trade that runs from Smith to Bastiat to Krugman. (Smith 1982; Bastiat 1996; Krugman 1998)

p.189, panel 3.   For an exploration of the Precautionary Principle, see Steel 2015. For a psychologically-minded critique of the Principle, see Sunstein 2005.

p.189, panel 4.   Carlyle 1855, p.448.

CHAPTER 8:
FANTASTIC JOURNEYS . . . AND HOW TO FINISH THEM

p.196, panels 3–4.   Cochrane 2011.

p.201.   For a brief history of the evolution of the European Union, see Cini and Borragán. 2016, pp.11–50.

p.203, panel 2.   Office for National Statistics 2012, Map 1.

p.203, panel 3.   Aisch et al. 2016.

p.206.   McCarthy 2017 provides data for 1966–2017; Brenan 2018 provides the latest update.

p.207, panel 2.   See ReasonTV 2014 for video of a panel featuring me, Mark Krikorian, and Alex Nowrasteh. For my reaction to this debate, see Caplan 2014f. In 2015, I debated Krikorian before the Social Contract Writers Workshop, an annual summit of anti-immigration organizations; see Caplan 2015b for my reaction.

p.208.   For background on the Overton Window, see Russell 2006.

p.209, panel 2.   The quote is from Allen 1971.

REFERENCES

Abramitzky, Ran, Leah Boustan, and Katherine Eriksson. 2012. "Europe's Tired, Poor, Huddled Masses: Self-Selection and Economic Outcomes in the Age of Mass Migration." *American Economic Review* 102(5), pp. 1832–1856.

Aisch, Gregor, Adam Pearce, and Karl Russell. 2016. "How Britain Voted in the EU Referendum." *New York Times*, June 24. URL https://www.nytimes.com/interactive/2016/06/24/world/europe/how-britain-voted-brexit-referendum.html.

Alba, Richard. 2004. "Language Assimilation Today: Bilingualism Persists More Than in the Past, but English Still Dominates." *Center for Comparative Immigration Studies Working Paper* #111. URL http://ccis.ucsd.edu/_files/wp111.pdf.

Alesina, Alberto, Edward Glaeser, and Bruce Sacerdote. 2001. "Why Doesn't the United States Have a European-Style Welfare State?" *Brookings Papers on Economic Activity* 2, pp. 187–277.

Alesina, Alberto, Armando Miano, and Stefanie Stantcheva. 2018. "Immigration and Redistribution." *NBER Working Paper* No. 24733. URL http://www.nber.org/papers/w24733.

Algan, Yann, and Pierre Cahuc. 2010. "Inherited Trust and Growth." *American Economic Review* 100(5), pp. 2060–92.

Algan, Yann, and Pierre Cahuc. 2014. "Trust, Growth, and Well-Being: New Evidence and Policy Implications." In Aghion, Philippe, and Steven Durlauf, eds. *Handbook of Economic Growth*, vol. 2. Oxford: North-Holland, pp. 49–120.

Allen, Woody. 1971. *Bananas*. URL http://www.script-o-rama.com/movie_scripts/b/bananas-script-transcript-woody-allen.html.

Bashir, Omar. 2015. "Testing Inferences about American Politics: A Review of the 'Oligarchy' Result." *Research and Politics* 2(4), pp. 1–7.

Bastiat, Frédéric. 1996. *Economic Sophisms*. Irvington-on-Hudson, NY: Foundation for Economic Education.

Bay, Ann-Helén, and Axel West Pedersen. 2006. "The Limits of Social Solidarity: Basic Income, Immigration and the Legitimacy of the Universal Welfare State." *Acta Sociologica* 49(4), pp. 419–436.

Berggren, Niclas, Mikael Elinder, and Henrik Jordahl. 2008. "Trust and Growth: A Shaky Relationship." *Empirical Economics* 35(2), pp. 251–274.

Bernstein, Peter. 1998. *Against the Gods: The Remarkable Story of Risk*. NY: John Wiley and Sons.

Bertoli, Simone, J. Fernández-Huertas Moraga, and Francesc Ortega. 2013. "Crossing the Border: Self-Selection, Earnings, and Individual Migration Decisions." *Journal of Development Economics* 101, pp. 75–91.

Bible Gateway. 2011a. "New International Version: Genesis 18: 20-32." URL https://www.biblegateway.com/passage/?search=Genesis+18%3A20-32&version=NIV.

Bible Gateway. 2011b. "New International Version: Luke 10: 30-37." URL https://www.biblegateway.com/passage/?search=Luke+10%3A30-10%3A37&version=NIV.

Bier, David. 2018. "U. S. Approves Far Fewer Muslim Refugees, Immigrants, & Travelers." *Cato at Liberty*, April 23. URL https://www.cato.org/blog/us-approves-far-fewer-muslim-refugees-immigrants-travelers.

Bjørnskov, Christian. 2007. "Determinants of Generalized Trust: A Cross-Country Comparison." *Public Choice* 130(1/2), pp. 1–21.

Blattman, Christopher, and Edward Miguel. 2010. "Civil War." *Journal of Economic Literature* 48(1), pp. 3–57.

Blau, Francine, and Christopher Mackie, eds. 2016. *The Economic and Fiscal Consequences of Immigration*. Washington, DC: National Academies Press. URL https://www.nap.edu/catalog/23550/the-economic-and-fiscal-consequences-of-immigration.

Bloom, Nicholas, and John van Reenen. 2010. "Why Do Management Practices Differ across Firms and Countries?" *Journal of Economic Perspectives* 24(1), pp. 203–224.

Booker, Salih, and William Minter. 2001. "Global Apartheid." *The Nation*, June 21. URL https://www.thenation.com/article/global-apartheid.

Borjas, George. 2001. *Heaven's Door: Immigration Policy and the American Economy*. Princeton, NJ: Princeton University Press.

Borjas, George. 2014. *Immigration Economics*. Cambridge, MA: Harvard University Press.

Borjas, George. 2015. "Immigration and Globalization: A Review Essay." *Journal of Economic Literature* 53(4), pp. 961–74.

Borjas, George. 2016. *We Wanted Workers: Unraveling the Immigration Narrative*. NY: W. W. Norton.

Borjas, George, and Lawrence Katz. 2007. "The Evolution of the Mexican-Born Workforce in the United States." In Borjas, George, ed. *Mexican Immigration to the United States*. Chicago: University of Chicago Press, pp. 13–55.

Brenan, Megan. 2018. "Record-High 75% of Americans Say Immigration Is Good Thing." *Gallup*, June 21. URL https://news.gallup.com/poll/235793/record-high-americans-say-immigration-good-thing.aspx.

Brimelow, Peter. 1995. *Alien Nation: Common Sense About America's Immigration Disaster*. NY: Random House.

Bureau of the Census. 1984. *1980 Census of Population*. Washington, DC: U.S. Government Printing Office. URL https://www2.census.gov/prod2/decennial/documents/1980/1980censusofpopu8011un_bw.pdf.

Bureau of the Census. 2018. "Household Type: 2015." *American FactFinder*.

Butler, Jeffrey, Paola Giuliano, and Luigi Guiso. 2016. "The Right Amount of Trust." *Journal of the European Economic Association* 14(5), pp. 1155–80.

Camarota, Steven, and Jessica Vaughan. 2009. "Immigration and Crime: Assessing a Conflicted Issue." *Center for Immigration Studies Backgrounder*, November. URL https://www.cis.org/sites/cis.org/files/articles/2009/crime.pdf.

Caplan, Bryan. 2005. "How Everyone Can Get Richer as Per-Capita Income Falls." *EconLog*, March 27. URL https://www.econlib.org/archives/2005/03/how_everyone_ca.html.

Caplan, Bryan. 2007. *The Myth of the Rational Voter: Why Democracies Choose Bad Policies*. Princeton, NJ: Princeton University Press.

Caplan, Bryan. 2008. "Milton Friedman Opposed a Pareto Improvement." *EconLog*, June 7. URL https://www.econlib.org/archives/2008/06/milton_friedman_10.html.

Caplan, Bryan. 2010. "You Don't Have to Raise the Average to Pull Your Weight." *EconLog*, September 17. URL https://www.econlib.org/archives/2010/09/you_dont_have_t.html.

Caplan, Bryan. 2011. *Selfish Reasons to Have More Kids: Why Being a Great Parent Is Less Work and More Fun Than You Think*. NY: Basic Books.

Caplan, Bryan. 2012a. "Some Unpleasant Immigration Arithmetic." *EconLog*, November 19. https://www.econlib.org/archives/2012/11/some_unpleasant.html.

Caplan, Bryan. 2012b. "Why Should We Restrict Immigration?" *Cato Journal* 32(1), pp. 5–24.

Caplan, Bryan. 2012c. "Immigration, Trespassing, and Socialism." *EconLog*, November 12. URL https://www.econlib.org/archives/2012/11/immigration_tre.html.

Caplan, Bryan. 2013a. "The Rights of the World's Poor: A Reply to Hassoun." *Cato Unbound*, March 19. URL https://www.cato-unbound.org/2013/03/19/bryan-caplan/rights-worlds-poor-reply-hassoun.

Caplan, Bryan. 2013b. "Let Anyone Take a Job Anywhere: My Opening Statement for IQ2." *EconLog*, November 1. URL http://www.econlib.org/archives/2013/11/let_anyone_take.html.

Caplan, Bryan. 2013c. "The Fine Line Between Social Darwinism and Suicidal Compassion." *EconLog*, June 6. URL https://www.econlib.org/archives/2013/06/my_hoover_immig.html.

Caplan, Bryan. 2013d. "Open Borders Is a Moderate Position." *EconLog*, September 3. URL https://www.econlib.org/archives/2013/09/the_golden_mean.html.

Caplan, Bryan. 2014a. "Trillion-Dollar Bills on the Sidewalk: The Borjas Critique." *EconLog*, July 16. URL https://www.econlib.org/archives/2014/07/open_borders_an_3.html.

Caplan, Bryan. 2014b. "Diasporas, Swamping, and Open Borders Abolitionism." *EconLog*, February 5. URL https://www.econlib.org/archives/2014/02/diasporas_swamp.html.

Caplan, Bryan. 2014c. "The Swamping that Wasn't: The Diaspora Dynamics of the Puerto Rican Open Borders Experiment." *EconLog*, March 27. URL https://www.econlib.org/archives/2014/03/the_swamping_th.html.

Caplan, Bryan. 2014d. "Meant for Each Other: Open Borders and Western Civilization." *EconLog*, May 7. URL https://www.econlib.org/archives/2014/05/meant_for_each.html.

Caplan, Bryan. 2014e. "A Hardy Weed: How Traditionalists Underestimate Western Civ." *Econlog,* June 23. URL https://www.econlib.org/archives/2014/06/a_hardy_week_ho.html.

Caplan, Bryan. 2014f. "Talking to Mark Krikorian." *EconLog*, April 24. URL https://www.econlib.org/archives/2014/04/talking_to_mark.html.

Caplan, Bryan. 2015a. "Demography and Decency." *EconLog*, December 15. URL https://www.econlib.org/archives/2015/12/demography_and.html.

Caplan, Bryan. 2015b. "What I Didn't Get to Say to Mark Krikorian." *EconLog*, October 26. URL https://www.econlib.org/archives/2015/10/what_i_didnt_ge.html.

Caplan, Bryan. 2016a. "Ancestry and Long-Run Growth Reading Club: Putterman and Weil." *EconLog*, January 27. URL https://www.econlib.org/archives/2016/01/ancestry_and_lo.html.

Caplan, Bryan. 2016b. "Ancestry and Long-Run Growth Reading Club: Comin, Easterly, and Gong." *EconLog*, February 3. URL https://www.econlib.org/archives/2016/02/ancestry_and_lo_1.html.

Caplan, Bryan. 2016c. "Ancestry and Long-Run Growth Reading Club: Spolaore and Wacziarg." *EconLog*, February 10. URL https://www.econlib.org/archives/2016/02/ancestry_and_lo_2.html.

Caplan, Bryan. 2016d. "Two Fun Facts from Putterman-Weil." *EconLog*, February 12. URL https://www.econlib.org/archives/2016/02/two_fun_facts_f.html.

Caplan, Bryan. 2016e. "National Origin as a Nurture Effect." *EconLog*, December 15. URL https://www.econlib.org/archives/2016/12/nationality_and.html.

Caplan, Bryan. 2017a. "Trust and Diversity: Not a Bang but a Whimper." *EconLog*, June 15. URL https://www.econlib.org/archives/2017/06/trust_and_diver.html.

Caplan, Bryan. 2017b. "Geography Is Policy." *EconLog*, May 15. URL https://www.econlib.org/archives/2017/05/geography_is_po.html.

Caplan, Bryan. 2017c. "The Wonder of International Adoption: Adult IQ in Sweden." *EconLog*, September 18. URL https://www.econlib.org/archives/2017/09/the_wonder_of_i.html.

Caplan, Bryan. 2017d. "The Wonder of International Adoption: High School Grades in Sweden." *EconLog*, September 20. URL https://www.econlib.org/archives/2017/09/the_wonder_of_i_1.html.

Caplan, Bryan. 2017e. "The Shining City on a Hill: Commentary on Reagan." *EconLog*, December 7. URL https://www.econlib.org/archives/2017/12/the_city_on_a_h.html.

Caplan, Bryan, and Stephen Miller. 2010. "Intelligence Makes People Think Like Economists: Evidence from the General Social Survey." *Intelligence* 38(6), pp. 636–647.

Caplan, Bryan, and Vipul Naik. 2015. "A Radical Case for Open Borders." In Powell, Benjamin, ed. *The Economics of Immigration: Market-Based Approaches, Social Science, and Public Policy.* Oxford: Oxford University Press, pp. 180–209.

Carens, Joseph. 1987. "Aliens and Citizens: The Case for Open Borders." *Review of Politics* 49(2), pp. 251–73.

Carlyle, Thomas, ed. 1855. *Oliver Cromwell's Letters and Speeches*, vol. 1. New York: Harper.

Carson, E. 2018. "Prisoners in 2016." *Bureau of Justice Statistics*, August 7. URL https://www.bjs. gov/content/pub/pdf/p16.pdf.

Chang, Howard. 2003. "Immigration and the Workplace: Immigration Restrictions as Employment Discrimination." *Chicago-Kent Law Review* 78, pp. 291–328.

Chua, Amy. 2011. *Battle Hymn of the Tiger Mother.* NY: Penguin Books.

Cini, Michelle, and Nieves Borragán, eds. 2016. *European Union Politics.* Oxford: Oxford University Press.

Clemens, Michael. 2011. "Economics and Emigration: Trillion-Dollar Bills on the Sidewalk?" *Journal of Economic Perspectives* 25(3), pp. 83–106.

Clemens, Michael, and Lant Pritchett. 2008. "Income per Natural: Measuring Development for People Rather Than Places." *Population and Development Review* 34(3), pp. 395-434.

Clemens, Michael, and Lant Pritchett. 2016. "The New Economic Case for Migration Restrictions: An Assessment." *Center for Global Development Working Paper #423.* URL https://papers. ssrn.com/sol3/papers. cfm?abstract _id=2630295.

Clemens, Michael, Claudio Montenegro, and Lant Pritchett. forthcoming. "The Place Premium: Bounding the Price Equivalent of Migration Barriers." *Review of Economics and Statistics.*

Clifton, Jon. 2013. "More Than 100 Million Worldwide Dream of Life in the U.S." *Gallup World*, March 21. URL https:// news. gallup.com/poll/161435/100-million-worldwide-dream-life.aspx.

Cochrane, Kira. 2011. "Jose Antonio Vargas: My Secret Life as an Undocumented US Immigrant." *The Guardian*, July 26. URL https://www.theguardian.com/world/2011/jul/26/jose-antonio-vargas-undocumented-immigrant.

Collier, Paul. 1999. "On the Economic Consequences of Civil War." *Oxford Economic Papers* 51(1), pp. 168-83.

Collier, Paul. 2013. *Exodus: How Migration Is Changing Our World.* NY: Oxford University Press.

Comin, Diego, William Easterly, and Erick Gong. 2010. "Was the Wealth of Nations Determined in 1000 BC?" *American Economic Journal: Macroeconomics* 2(3): 65-97.

Congressional Budget Office. 2018. "The 2018 Long-Term Budget Outlook." URL https://www.cbo.gov/system/files?file=2018-06/53919-2018ltbo.pdf.

Connor, Phillip, D'Vera Cohn, and Ana Gonzalez-Barrera. 2013. "Changing Patterns of Global Migration and Remittances." *Pew Research Center*, December 17. URL http://www.pewsocialtrends.org/2013/12/17/changing-patterns-of-global-migration-and-remittances.

Cortés, Patricia, and José Tessada. 2011. "Low-Skilled Immigration and the Labor Supply of Highly Skilled Women." *American Economic Journal: Applied Economics* 3(3), pp. 88-123.

Coulter, Ann. 2015a. *¡Adios, America!: The Left's Plan to Turn Our Country Into a Third World Hellhole.* Washington, DC: Regnery.

Coulter, Ann. 2015b. December 22. URL https://www.facebook.com/OfficialAnnCoulter/posts/which-reminds-me-low-iq-immigrants-are-lowering-your-income-your-freedom-your-wa/802900983153051.

Cowen, Tyler, and Alex Tabarrok. 2018. *Modern Principles of Economics*, 4th edition. NY: Macmillan Learning.

D'Amuri, Francesco, and Giovanni Peri. 2014. "Immigration, Jobs, and Employment Protection: Evidence from Europe Before and During the Great Recession." *Journal of the European Economic Association* 12(2), pp. 432–464.

Dalen, Monica, Anders Hyern, Frank Lindblad, Anna Odenstad, Finn Rasmussen, and Bo Vinnerljung. 2008. "Educational Attainment and Cognitive Competence in Adopted Men: A Study of International and National Adoptees, Siblings and a General Swedish Population." *Children and Youth Services Review* 30(10), pp. 1211–9.

Delogu, Marco, Frédéric Docquier, and Joël Machado. 2018. "Globalizing Labor and the World Economy: The Role of Human Capital." *Journal of Economic Growth* 23(2), pp. 223–258.

Derbyshire, John. 2015. "John Derbyshire On Why Race Realism Makes More Sense Than 'Magic Dirt' Theory." *VDARE .com*, November 1. URL https://vdare.com/articles/john-derbyshire-on-why-race-realism-makes-more-sense -than-magic-dirt-theory.

Diehl, Claudia, and Andreas Wüst. 2010. "Voter Turnout Amongst Immigrants and Visible Minorities in Comparative Perspective." In Bird, Karen, Thomas Saalfeld, and Andreas Wüst, eds. *The Political Representation of Immigrants and Minorities: Voters, Parties and Parliaments in Liberal Democracies*. London: Routledge, pp. 25–65.

Dinesen, Peter. 2012. "Does Generalized (Dis)Trust Travel? Examining the Impact of Cultural Heritage and Destination-Country Environment on Trust of Immigrants." *Political Psychology* 33(4), pp. 495–511.

Dinesen, Peter, and Marc Hooghe. 2010. "When in Rome, Do as the Romans Do: The Acculturation of Generalized Trust among Immigrants in Western Europe." *International Migration Review* 44(3), pp. 697–727.

Disaster Center. 2017. "United States Crime Rates 1960-2016." URL http://www.disastercenter.com/crime/uscrime.htm.

Donno, Daniela, and Bruce Russett. 2004. "Islam, Authoritarianism, and Female Empowerment: What Are the Linkages?" *World Politics* 56(4), pp. 582–607.

Drury, A. Cooper, Jonathan Krieckhaus, and Michael Lusztig. 2006. "Corruption, Democracy, and Economic Growth." *International Political Science Review* 27(2), pp. 121–136.

Esipova, Neli, Anita Pugliese, and Julie Ray. 2017. "Potential Net Migration Index Falls in Middle East, Latin America." *Gallup World*, June 20. URL https://news.gallup.com/poll/212141/potential-net-migration-falls-middle-east -latin-america.aspx.

Esipova, Neli, and Julie Ray. 2012. "More Adults Would Move for Temporary Work Than Permanently." *Gallup World*, March 9. URL http://www.gallup.com/poll/153182/Adults-Move-Temporary-Work-Permanently.aspx.

Esipova, Neli, Rajesh Srinivasan, and Julie Ray. 2009. "Potential Net Migration Could Change Nations." *Gallup World*, November 6. URL http://www.gallup.com/poll/124193/potential-net-migration-change-developed-nations.aspx.

Esipova, Neli, Rajesh Srinivasan, and Julie Ray. 2014. "Potential Net Migration Index Declines in Many Countries." *Gallup World*, January 17. URL http://www.gallup.com/poll/166796/potential-net-migration-index-declines -countries.aspx.

Espinoza, Robert. 2017. "Immigrants and the Direct Care Workforce." *PHI*, June. URL https://phinational.org/wp -content/uploads/2017/06/immigrants_and_the_direct_care_workforce_-_phi_-_june_2017.pdf.

FindLaw. 2018. "Gonzales v. Williams." URL https://caselaw. findlaw.com/us-supreme-court/192/1.html.

Fish, M. 2002. "Islam and Authoritarianism." *World Politics* 55(1), pp. 4-37.

Friedman, Milton. 1999. "Q&A With Milton Friedman." ISIL Interview.

Gallup, John, Jeffrey Sachs, and Andrew Mellinger. 1999. "Geography and Economic Development." *International Regional Science Review* 22(2): 179–232.

Gerber, David. 2011. *American Immigration: A Very Short Introduction*. NY: Oxford University Press.

Gibson, John, and David McKenzie. 2011. "Eight Questions about Brain Drain." *Journal of Economic Perspectives* 25(3), pp. 107–28.

Gilens, Martin. 2012. *Affluence and Influence: Economic Inequality and Political Power in America*. Princeton, NJ: Princeton University Press and Russell Sage Foundation.

Gjelten, Tom. 2015. *A Nation of Nations: A Great American Immigration Story*. NY: Simon and Schuster.

Glaeser, Edward. 2017. "Reforming Land Use Regulations." *Brookings Center on Regulation and Markets Report*, April 24. URL https://www.brookings. edu/research/reforming-land-use-regulations.

Glaeser, Edward, David Laibson, Jose Scheinkman, and Christine Soutter. 2000. "Measured Trust." *Quarterly Journal of Economics* 115(3), pp. 811–46.

Gochenour, Zachary, and Alex Nowrasteh. 2014. "The Political Externalities of Immigration: Evidence from the United States." *Cato Working Paper*, January 15. URL https://object.cato.org/sites/cato.org/files/pubs/pdf/working -paper-14-3.pdf.

Gonzalez, Libertad, and Ortega, Francesc. 2013. "Immigration and Housing Booms: Evidence from Spain." *Journal of Regional Science* 53(1), pp. 37–59.

Gottfredsen, Linda. 1994. "Mainstream Science on Intelligence: An Editorial With 52 Signatories, History, and Bibliography." *Intelligence* 24(1), pp. 13–23.

Gwartney, James, Robert Lawson, and Joshua Hall. 2017. *Economic Freedom of the World: 2017 Annual Report.* Fraser Institute. URL https://www.fraserinstitute.org/sites/default/files/economic-freedom-of-the-world-2017.pdf.

Habila, Helon. 2016. *The Chibok Girls: The Boko Haram Kidnappings and Islamist Militancy in Nigeria.* NY: Columbia Global Reports.

Hamilton, Bob, and John Whalley. 1984. "Efficiency and Distributional Implications of Global Restrictions on Labour Mobility: Calculations and Policy Implications." *Journal of Development Economics* 14(1), pp. 61–75.

Harford, Tim. 2012. *The Undercover Economist: Exposing Why the Rich Are Rich, the Poor Are Poor—and Why You Can Never Buy a Decent Used Car!* Oxford: Oxford University Press.

Harris, Judith. 2009. *The Nurture Assumption: Why Children Turn Out the Way They Do.* NY: Free Press.

Hauser, Christine. 2016. "Donald Trump Jr. Compares Syrian Refugees to Skittles That 'Would Kill You.'" *New York Times*, September 20. URL https://www.nytimes.com/2016/09/21/us/politics/donald-trump-jr-faces-backlash-after-comparing-syrian-refugees-to-skittles-that-can-kill.html.

Havocscope. 2018. "Prices Charged by Human Smugglers." URL https://www.havocscope.com/black-market-prices/human-smuggling-fees.

Hendricks, Lutz. 2002. "How Important Is Human Capital for Development? Evidence from Immigrant Earnings." *American Economic Review* 92(1), pp. 198–219.

Herrnstein, Richard, and Mark Snyderman. 1983. "Intelligence Tests and the Immigration Act of 1924." *American Psychologist* 38(9), pp. 986–995.

Howley, Kerry. 2008. "Ending Global Apartheid." *Reason*, February. URL http://reason.com/archives/2008/01/24/ending-global-apartheid/singlepage.

Huemer, Michael. 2010. "Is There a Right to Immigrate?" *Social Theory and Practice* 36(3), pp. 429–61.

Huemer, Michael. 2013. *The Problem of Political Authority: An Examination of the Right to Coerce and the Duty to Obey.* NY: Palgrave Macmillan.

Institute for the Study of Western Civilization. 2014. "Debate on Immigration: Should the United States Significantly Liberalize Immigration?" URL http://www.depts.ttu.edu/westernciv/videos_others/debate_immigration.php.

International Organization for Migration. 2017. *World Migration Report 2018.* Geneva, Switzerland: International Organization for Migration. URL https://publications.iom.int/system/files/pdf/wmr_2018_en.pdf.

IQ Research. 2018. "World Ranking of Countries by Their Average IQ." URL https://iq-research.info/en/average-iq-by-country.

Iregui, Ana Maria. 2005. "Efficiency Gains from the Elimination of Global Restrictions on Labour Mobility." In Borjas, George, and Jeff Crisp, eds. *Poverty, International Migration and Asylum.* NY: Palgrave Macmillan, pp. 211–38.

Jensen, Arthur. 1998. *The g Factor: The Science of Mental Ability.* Westport, CT: Praeger.

Johns Hopkins Medicine. 2018. "Minimally Invasive Surgery: Types of Minimally Invasive Surgery." *HopkinsMedicine.* URL https://www.hopkinsmedicine.org/minimally_invasive_robotic_surgery/types.html.

Johnson, Jenna. 2015. "Trump Calls for 'Total and Complete Shutdown of Muslims Entering the United States.'" *Washington Post*, December 7. URL https://www.washingtonpost.com/news/post-politics/wp/2015/12/07/donald-trump-calls-for-total-and-complete-shutdown-of-muslims-entering-the-united-states/?utm_term=.d64a2406d24c.

Jones, Garett. 2015. "Will Open Borders Change Your Nation's SAT Score?" URL http://mason.gmu.edu/~gjonesb/OpenBordersSacrifice.pptx.

Jones, Garett. 2016. *Hive Mind: How Your Nation's IQ Matters So Much More Than Your Own.* Stanford, CA: Stanford University Press.

Jones, Garett. 2017. "Are the Global Benefits of Open Borders a Fallacy of Composition? Three Examples." URL https://www.dropbox.com/s/sdtrfig2vu81b8y/FallacyOfCompositionBeamerNUSFinal.pdf?dl=0.

Jones, Garett, and W. Schneider. 2006. "Intelligence, Human Capital, and Economic Growth: A Bayesian Averaging of Classical Estimates (BACE) Approach." *Journal of Economic Growth* 11(1), pp. 71–93.

Juffer, Femmie, and Marinus van IJzendoorn. 2009. "International Adoption Comes of Age: Development of International Adoptees from a Longitudinal and Meta-Analytical Perspective." In Wrobel, Gretchen, and Elsbeth Neil, eds. *International Advances in Adoption Research for Practice*. Chichester, UK: Wiley-Blackwell, pp. 169–192.

Junn, Jane, Taeku Lee, S. Ramakrishnan, and Janelle Wong. 2011. "Asian American Public Opinion." In Edwards, George, Lawrence Jacobs, and Robert Shapiro, eds. *The Oxford Handbook of American Public Opinion and the Media*. Oxford: Oxford University Press, pp. 520–34.

Kahneman, Daniel. 2011. *Thinking, Fast and Slow*. NY: Farrar, Straus, and Giroux.

Kant, Immanuel. 1887. *The Philosophy of Law: An Exposition of the Fundamental Principles of Jurisprudence as the Science of Right*. Edinburgh, UK: T&T Clark.

Kennan, John. 2013. "Open Borders." *Review of Economic Dynamics* 16(2), pp. L1–L13.

Kievit, Rogier, Willem Frankenhuis, Lourens Waldorp, and Denny Borsboom. 2013. "Simpson's Paradox in Psychological Science: A Practical Guide." *Frontiers in Psychology* 4, pp. 1–14.

Kim, Dongbin, Susan Twombly, and Lisa Wolf-Wendel. 2012. "International Faculty in American Universities: Experiences of Academic Life, Productivity, and Career Mobility." *New Directions in Institutional Research* 155, pp. 27–46.

King, Martin Luther. 1963. "I Have a Dream..." *National Archives*. URL https://www.archives.gov/files/press/exhibits/dream-speech.pdf.

Klein, Paul, and Gustavo Ventura. 2009. "Productivity Differences and the Dynamic Effects of Labor Movements." *Journal of Monetary Economics* 56(8), pp. 1059–73.

Knoema. 2018. "United States of America: Crude Death Rate." URL https://knoema.com/atlas/United-States-of-America/Death-rate.

"Know-Nothing." c. 1850. URL https://public-media.smithsonianmag.com/filer/fc/2d/fc2d8316-33df-49ee-b171-3b9a52545564/cwbwma. jpg.

Kotwal, Ashok, Bharat Ramaswami, and Wilima Wadhwa. 2011. "Economic Liberalization and Indian Economic Growth: What's the Evidence?" *Journal of Economic Literature* 49(4), pp. 1152–99.

Krikorian, Mark. 2008. *The New Case Against Immigration: Both Legal and Illegal*. NY: Sentinel.

Krikorian, Mark. 2010. *How Obama Is Transforming America Through Immigration*. NY: Encounter Books.

Krugman, Paul. 1998. *The Accidental Theorist: And Other Dispatches from the Dismal Science*. NY: W. W. Norton.

Krugman, Paul, and Robin Wells. 2017. *Essentials of Economics*, 4th edition. NY: Macmillan Learning.

Kuran, Timur, and Cass Sunstein. 1999. "Availability Cascades and Risk Regulation." *Stanford Law Review* 51(4), pp. 683–768.

Lee, Kwan Yew. 2000. *From the Third World to the First: The Singapore Story 1965-2000*. NY: HarperCollins.

Lee, Matthew, and Ramiro Martinez. 2009. "Immigration Reduces Crime: An Emerging Scholarly Consensus." *Sociology of Crime, Law and Deviance* 13, pp. 3–16.

Legrain, Philippe. 2007. *Immigrants: Your Country Needs Them*. Princeton, NJ: Princeton University Press.

Ludmerer, Kenneth. 1972. "Genetics, Eugenics, and the Immigration Restriction Act of 1924." *Bulletin of the History of Medicine* 46(1), pp. 59–81.

Lynn, Richard, and Gerhard Meisenberg. 2010. "National IQs Calculated and Validated for 108 Nations." *Intelligence* 38(4), pp. 353–60.

Lynn, Richard, and Tatu Vanhanen. 2002. *IQ and the Wealth of Nations*. Westport, CT: Praeger.

Maddison Project Database. 2018. URL https://www.rug.nl/ggdc/historicaldevelopment/maddison/releases/maddison-project-database-2018.

"The Magic Washer." 1886. URL https://www.loc.gov/resource/pga.02758.

Mankiw, N. Gregory. 2015. *Principles of Economics*, 7th edition. Stamford, CT: Cengage Learning.

Mansbridge, Jane. 1990. *Beyond Self-Interest*. Chicago: University of Chicago Press.

Matthews, Dylan. 2016. "Remember that Study Saying America Is an Oligarchy? 3 Rebuttals Say It's Wrong." *Vox*, May 9. URL https://www.vox.com/2016/5/9/11502464/gilens-page-oligarchy-study.

McCarthy, Justin. 2017. "Overall U.S. Desire to Decrease Immigration Unchanged in 2017." *Gallup*, June 27. URL https://news.gallup.com/poll/212846/overall-desire-decrease-immigration-unchanged-2017.aspx.

McKenzie, David, Steven Stillman, and John Gibson. 2010. "How Important Is Selection? Experimental vs. Non-Experimental Measures of the Income Gains from Migration." *Journal of the European Economic Association* 8(4), pp. 913–45.

Migration Policy Institute. 2016. "Age-Sex Pyramids of U. S. Immigrants and Native-Born Populations, 1970–Present." URL https://www.migrationpolicy.org/programs/data-hub/charts/age-sex-pyramids-immigrant-and-native-born-population-over-time.

Mishkin, Frederic. 2016. *The Economics of Money, Banking, and Financial Markets.* Boston: Pearson.

Mo, Pak-Hung. 2001. "Corruption and Economic Growth." *Journal of Comparative Economics* 29(1), pp. 66–79.

Moses, Jonathon, and Bjorn Letnes. 2004. "The Economic Costs to International Labor Restrictions: Revisiting the Empirical Discussion." *World Development,* 32(10), pp. 1609–26.

Moses, Jonathon, and Bjorn Letnes. 2005. "If People Were Money: Estimating the Gains and Scope of Free Migration." In Borjas, George, and Jeff Crisp, eds. *Poverty, International Migration and Asylum.* NY: Palgrave Macmillan, pp. 188–210.

Naik, Vipul. 2018a. "Political Externalities." *Open Borders: The Case.* URL https://openborders.info/political-externalities.

Naik, Vipul. 2018b. "Keyhole Solutions." *Open Borders: The Case.* URL https://openborders.info/keyhole-solutions.

Nannestad, Peter. 2008. "What Have We Learned About Generalized Trust, If Anything?" *Annual Review of Political Science* 11, pp. 413–36.

Nast, Thomas. 1871. "The Usual Irish Way of Doing Things." URL https://library.osu.edu/dc/concern/generic_works/g732x041f.

National Museum of American History. 2018a. "Legacy of the Bracero Program." *Bittersweet Harvest: The Bracero Program 1942-1964.* URL http://americanhistory.si.edu/bracero/legacy.

National Museum of American History. 2018b. "Japs Keep Moving – This Is a White Man's Neighborhood." *A More Perfect Union: Japanese Americans and the U. S. Constitution.* URL https://amhistory. si. edu/perfectunion/collection/image.asp?ID=411.

National Weather Service. 2018. "How Dangerous Is Lightning?" URL https://www.weather.gov/safety/lightning-odds.

Newport, Frank. 2018. "Immigration Surges to Top of Most Important Problem List." *Gallup*, July 18. URL https://news. gallup.com/poll/237389/immigration-surges-top-important-problem-list.aspx.

Ngai, Mae. 1999. "The Architecture of Race in American Immigration Law: A Reexamination of the Immigration Act of 1924." *Journal of American History* 86(1), pp. 67-92.

Nowrasteh, Alex. 2015. "Immigrant Crime: What the Research Says." *Cato at Liberty*, July 14. URL https://www.cato.org/blog/immigration-crime-what-research-says.

Nowrasteh, Alex. 2016. "Terrorism and Immigration: A Risk Analysis." *Cato Institute Policy Analysis*, September 13. URL https://object.cato.org/sites/cato.org/files/pubs/pdf/pa798_2.pdf.

Nowrasteh, Alex, and Sophie Cole. 2013. "Building a Wall Around the Welfare State, Instead of the Country." *Policy Analysis* 732, July 25. URL https://object.cato.org/sites/cato.org/files/pubs/pdf/pa732_web_1.pdf.

Nowrasteh, Alex, and Sam Wilson. 2017. "Immigrants Assimilate Into the Political Mainstream." *Cato Institute Economic Development Bulletin* 27, January 19. URL https://object.cato.org/sites/cato.org/files/pubs/pdf/edb_27.pdf.

Nunn, Nathan, and Leonard Wantchekon. 2011. "The Slave Trade and the Origin of Mistrust in Africa." *American Economic Review* 101(7), pp. 3221–3252.

Odenstad, Anna, Anders Hyern, Frank Lindblad, Finn Rasmussen, Bo Vinnerljung, and Monica Dalen. 2008. "Does Age at Adoption and Geographic Origin Matter? A National Cohort Study of Cognitive Test Performance in Adult Inter-Country Adoptees." *Psychological Medicine* 38(12), pp. 1803–14.

Office for National Statistics. 2012. "International Migrants in England and Wales: 2011." December 11. URL https://www.ons. gov. uk/peoplepopulationandcommunity/populationandmigration/internationalmigration/articles/internationalmigrantsinenglandandwales/2012-12-11.

Office of Management and Budget. 2017. *Historical Tables: Budget of the U.S. Government*. Washington, DC: Government Publishing Office. URL https://www.govinfo.gov/content/pkg/BUDGET-2017-TAB/pdf/BUDGET -2017-TAB.pdf.

Office of the Assistant Secretary for Planning and Evaluation. 2009. "Summary of Immigrant Eligibility Restrictions Under Current Law." *APSE*, February 25. URL https://aspe.hhs.gov/basic-report/summary-immigrant -eligibility-restrictions-under-current-law.

Ortiz-Ospina, Esteban, and Max Roser. 2017. "Trust." *OurWorldInData.org*. URL https://ourworldindata.org/trust.

Ottaviano, Gianmarco, and Giovanni Peri. 2006. "The Economic Value of Cultural Diversity: Evidence from U. S. Cities." *Journal of Economic Geography* 6(1), pp. 9–44.

Ottaviano, Gianmarco, and Giovanni Peri. 2012. "Rethinking the Effect of Immigration on Wages." *Journal of the European Economic Association* 10(1), pp. 152–197.

Parker, A. Warner. 1924. "The Quota Provisions of the Immigration Act of 1924." *American Journal of International Law* 18(4), pp. 737–754.

Peri, Giovanni, and Chad Sparber. 2009. "Task Specialization, Immigration, and Wages." *American Economic Journal: Applied Economics* 1(3), pp. 135–169.

Pew Research Center. 2017. "Indians in the U.S. Fact Sheet." *Social and Demographic Trends*, September 8. URL http://www.pewsocialtrends.org/fact-sheet/asian-americans-indians-in-the-u-s.

Plato. 2002. *Five Dialogues: Euthyphro, Apology, Crito, Meno, Phaedo*. Indianapolis, IN: Hackett Publishing.

Posner, Richard. 1979. "Utilitarianism, Economics, and Legal Theory." *Journal of Legal Studies* 8(1), pp. 103–140.

Posner, Richard. 1980. "The Ethical and Political Basis of the Efficiency Norm in Common Law Adjudication." *Hofstra Law Review* 8(3), pp. 487–507.

Posner, Richard. 2003. *Law, Pragmatism, and Democracy*. Cambridge, MA: Harvard University Press.

Pritchett, Lant. 2006. *Let Their People Come: Breaking the Gridlock on International Labor Mobility*. Washington, DC: Center for Global Development.

Pritchett, Lant, Clifford Gaddy, and Simon Johnson. 2006. "Boom Towns and Ghost Countries: Geography, Agglomeration, and Population Mobility." *Brookings Trade Forum: Global Labor Markets?*, pp. 1–56.

Putnam, Robert. 2007. "E Pluribus Unum: Diversity and Community in the Twenty-first Century." *Scandinavian Political Studies* 30(2), pp. 137–74.

Putterman, Louis, and David Weil. 2010. "Post-1500 Population Flows and the Long-Run Determinants of Economic Growth and Inequality." *Quarterly Journal of Economics* 125(4): 1627–1682.

Quote Investigator. 2015. "People Who Say It Cannot Be Done Should Not Interrupt Those Who Are Doing It." URL http://quoteinvestigator.com/2015/01/26/doing.

Ratha, Dilip, Sonia Plaza, Hanspeter Wyss, Supriyo De, Kirsten Schuettler, and Soonhwa Yi. 2006. "Trends in Remittances, 2016: A New Normal of Slow Growth." *People Move*, October 6. URL http://blogs.worldbank.org/peoplemove/trends-remittances-2016-new-normal-slow-growth.

Ratiner, Susan, ed. 2015. *The Poems of Emma Lazarus, vol. 1*. NY: Dover Publications.

Reagan, Ronald. 1987. "Remarks on East-West Relations at the Brandenburg Gate in West Berlin." *American Presidency Project*, June 12. URL https://www.presidency.ucsb.edu/documents/remarks-east-west-relations -the-brandenburg-gate-west-berlin.

Reagan, Ronald. 1989. "Farewell Address to the Nation." *American Presidency Project*, January 11. URL http://www.presidency.ucsb.edu/ws/index.php?pid=29650.

ReasonTV. 2014. "Should America Open Its Borders?" May 11. URL https://www.youtube.com/watch?v=yUrJkweaw34.

Redden, Elizabeth. 2015. "Fee for Being Foreign." *Inside Higher Ed*, May 8. URL https://www.insidehighered.com/news/2015/05/08/some-public-universities-are-charging-differentiated-tuition-rates-or-raising-fees.

Rindermann, Heiner. 2018. *Cognitive Capitalism: Human Capital and the Well-Being of Nations*. Cambridge: Cambridge University Press.

Rindermann, Heiner, Michael Sailer, and James Thompson. 2009. "The Impact of Smart Fractions, Cognitive Ability of Politicians and Average Competence of Peoples on Social Development." *Talent Development & Excellence* 1(1), pp. 3–25.

Roberts, Bryan, Edward Alden, and John Whitley. 2013. "Managing Illegal Immigration to the United States: How Effective Is Enforcement?" *Council on Foreign Relations*, May. URL https://cfrd8-files.cfr.org/sites/default/files/book_pdf/Managing_Illegal_Immigration_report%20%282%29.pdf.

Roberts, Bryan, Gordon Hanson, Derekh Cornwell, and Scott Borger. 2010. "An Analysis of Migrant Smuggling Costs along the Southwest Border." *Office of Immigration Statistics Working Paper*. URL https://www.dhs.gov/xlibrary/assets/statistics/publications/ois-smuggling-wp.pdf.

Roth, Felix. 2009. "Does Too Much Trust Hamper Economic Growth?" *Kyklos* 62(1), pp. 103–28.

Rumbaut, Rubén, Douglas Massey, and Frank Bean. 2006. "Linguistic Life Expectancies: Immigration Language Retention in Southern California." *Population and Development Review* 32(3), pp. 447–60.

Russell, Nathan. 2006. "An Introduction to the Overton Window of Political Possibilities." *Mackinac Center for Public Policy*, January 4. URL https://www.mackinac.org/7504.

Ryan, Camille. 2013. "Language Use in the United States: 2011." *American Community Survey Reports*, August. URL https://www2.census.gov/library/publications/2013/acs/acs-22/acs-22.pdf.

Sá, Filipa. 2015. "Immigration and House Prices in the UK." *Economic Journal* 125(587), pp. 1393–1424.

Sachs, Jeffrey. 2003. "Institutions Matter, but Not for Everything." *Finance and Development*, June, pp. 38–41.

Sachs, Jeffrey, and Andrew Warner. 1995a. "Economic Convergence and Economic Policies." *NBER Working Paper* No. 5039. National Bureau of Economic Research, Cambridge, MA.

Sachs, Jeffrey, and Andrew Warner. 1995b. "Economic Reform and the Process of Global Integration." *Brookings Papers on Economic Activity* 1, 1–95.

Sachs, Jeffrey, and Wing Woo. 2001. "Understanding China's Economic Performance." *Journal of Policy Reform* 4(1), pp. 1–50.

Saiz, Albert. 2007. "Immigration and Housing Rents in American Cities." *Journal of Urban Economics* 61(2), pp. 345–371.

Saiz, Albert, and Susan Wachter. 2011. "Immigration and the Neighborhood." *American Economic Journal: Economic Policy* 3(2), pp. 169–188.

Salam, Reihan. 2018. *Melting Pot or Civil War? A Son of Immigrants Makes the Case Against Open Borders*. NY: Sentinel.

Sankhe, Shirish, Ireena Vittal, Richard Dobbs, Ajit Mohan, Ankur Gulati, Jonathan Ablett, Shishir Gupta, Alex Kim, Sudipto Paul, Aditya Sanghvi, and Gurpreet Sethy. 2010. *India's Urban Awakening: Building Inclusive Cities, Sustaining Economic Growth*. McKinsey Global Institute, April. URL https://www.mckinsey.com/~/media/McKinsey/Featured%20Insights/Urbanization/Urban%20awakening%20in%20India/MGI_Indias_urban_awakening_full_report. ashx.

Schoenberg, Arnold. 1950. *Style and Idea*. NY: Philosophical Library.

Schubert, Louis, Thomas Dye, and Harmon Zeigler. 2015. *The Irony of Democracy: An Uncommon Introduction to American Politics*. Boston, MA: Cengage Learning.

Schwarz, Anita, and Omar Arias. 2014. *The Inverting Pyramid: Pension Systems Facing Demographic Challenges in Europe and Central Asia*. Washington, DC: The World Bank. URL https://elibrary.worldbank.org/doi/pdf/10.1596/978-0-8213-9908-8.

Segal, Nancy. 2000. *Entwined Lives: Twins and What They Tell Us About Human Behavior*. NY: Penguin Group.

Smith, Adam. 1982. *An Inquiry Into the Nature and Causes of the Wealth of Nations*. Indianapolis, IN: Liberty Fund.

Smith, Nathanael. 2010. *Principles of a Free Society*. Fairfax, VA: John Locke Institute.

Smith, Nathanael. 2012. "Robots or Immigrants?" *Open Borders: The Case*, December 15. URL https://openborders.info/blog/robots-or-immigrants.

Snopes. 2018. "William Sutton—'That's Where the Money Is.'" URL https://www.snopes.com/fact-check/willie-sutton.

Snyder, Thomas, Cristobal de Brey, and Sally Dillow. 2018. *Digest of Education Statistics 2016*. Washington, DC: National Center for Education Statistics. URL https://nces.ed.gov/pubs2017/2017094.pdf.

Soroka, Stuart, Keith Banting, and Richard Johnston. 2006. "Immigration and Redistribution in a Global Era." In Bardhan, Pranab, Samuel Bowles, and Michael Wallerstein, eds. *Globalization and Egalitarian Redistribution.* Princeton, NJ: Princeton University Press.

Spolaore, Enrico, and Romain Wacziarg. 2013. "How Deep Are the Roots of Economic Development?" *Journal of Economic Literature* 51(2): 325–369.

Steel, Daniel. 2015. *Philosophy and the Precautionary Principle: Science, Evidence, and Environmental Policy.* Cambridge: Cambridge University Press.

Stepan, Alfred, and Graeme Robertson. 2003. "An 'Arab' More Than a 'Muslim' Democracy Gap." *Journal of Democracy* 14(3), pp. 30–34.

Stevens, Gillian. 1999. "Age at Immigration and Second Language Proficiency Among Foreign-Born Adults." *Language in Society* 28, pp. 555–578.

Stevens, Gillian. 2015. "Trajectories of English Acquisition Among Foreign-Born Spanish-Language Children in the United States." *International Migration Review* 49(4), pp. 981–1000.

Sunstein, Cass. 2005. *The Laws of Fear: Beyond the Precautionary Principle.* Cambridge: Cambridge University Press.

Tabarrok, Alexander. 2000. "Economic and Moral Factors in Favor of Open Immigration." *Independent Institute,* September 14. URL http://www.independent.org/issues/article. asp?id=486.

Taylor, Frederick. 2008. *The Berlin Wall: A World Divided, 1961–1989.* NY: HarperCollins.

Trump, Donald. 2016. "Remarks on Foreign Policy at the National Press Club in Washington, DC." *American Presidency Project,* April 27. URL http://www.presidency. ucsb. edu/ws/index. php?pid=117813.

USCIS 2017. "H-1B Specialty Occupations, DOD Cooperative Research and Development Project Workers, and Fashion Models." URL https: //www.uscis.gov/working-united-states/temporary-workers/h-1b-specialty-occupations -dod-cooperative-research-and-development-project-workers-and-fashion-models.

USCIS 2018a. "H-2A Temporary Agricultural Workers." URL https://www.uscis.gov/working-united-states/ temporary-workers/h-2a-temporary-agricultural-workers.

USCIS 2018b. "H-2B Temporary Non-Agricultural Workers." URL https://www.uscis.gov/working-united-states/ temporary-workers/h-2b-temporary-non-agricultural-workers.

United States Census Bureau 2018a. "QuickFacts: Los Angeles County, California." U.S. Department of Commerce. URL https://www.census.gov/quickfacts/fact/table/losangelescountycalifornia/PST045217.

United States Census Bureau 2018b. "Characteristics of the Group Quarters Population by Group Quarters Type." *American FactFinder.*

United States Sentencing Commission. 2017. "Quick Facts: Illegal Reentry Statistics." URL https://www.ussc.gov/sites/ default/files/pdf/research-and-publications/quick-facts/Illegal_Reentry_FY17.pdf.

USA.gov. 2018. "How to Apply for U.S. Citizenship." URL https://www.usa.gov/become-us-citizen.

USGovernmentSpending.com. 2018. "Government Spending Details." URL https://www.usgovernmentspending.com/ year_spending_2015USBn_19bs2n_101713401200#usgs302.

Uslaner, Eric. 2008. "Where You Stand Depends on Where Your Grandparents Sat: The Inheritability of Generalized Trust." *Public Opinion Quarterly* 72(4), pp. 725–40.

Van der Vossen, Bas, and Jason Brennan. 2018. *In Defense of Openness: Why Global Freedom Is the Humane Solution to Global Poverty.* Oxford: Oxford University Press.

Van IJzendoorn, Marinus, Femmie Juffer, and Caroline Poelhuis. 2005. "Adoption and Cognitive Development: A Meta-Analytic Comparison of Adopted and Nonadopted Children's IQ and School Performance." *Psychological Bulletin* 131(2), pp. 301-16.

Van IJzendoorn, Marinus, Marian Bakermans-Kranenburg, and Femmie Juffer. 2007. "Plasticity of Growth in Height, Weight, and Head Circumference: Meta-Analytic Evidence of Massive Catch-Up After International Adoption." *Journal of Developmental and Behavioral Pediatrics* 28(4), pp. 334–43.

Van Zanden, Jan, Joerg Baten, Marco d'Ercole, Auke Rijpma, Conal Smith, and Marcel Timmer, eds. 2014. *How Was Life?: Global Well-Being Since 1820.* OECD Publishing. URL https://www.oecd-ilibrary.org/how-was -life_5jz41pwdz5zn.pdf?itemId=%2Fcontent%2Fpublication%2F9789264214262-en&mimewType=pdf.

Vigdor, Jacob. 2015. "The Civic and Cultural Assimilation of Immigrants to the United States." In Powell, Benjamin, ed. *The Economics of Immigration: Market-Based Approaches, Social Science, and Public Policy*. Oxford: Oxford University Press, pp. 70–91.

Vinnerljung, Bo, Frank Linkblad, Anders Hyern, Finn Rasmussen, and Monica Dalen. 2010. "School Performance at Age 16 Among International Adoptees: A Swedish National Cohort Study." *International Social Work* 53(4), pp. 510–527.

Voltaire, Francois. 1980. *Letters on England*. London: Penguin Classics.

Wagner, Clifford. 1982. "Simpson's Paradox in Real Life." *American Statistician* 36(1), pp. 46–8.

Waters, Mary, and Marisa Pineau, eds. 2015. *The Integration of Immigrants Into American Society*. Washington, DC: National Academies Press.

Whalen, Carmen. 2005. "Colonialism, Citizenship, and the Making of the Puerto Rican Diaspora: An Introduction." In Whalen, Carmen, and Víctor Vázquez-Hernández, eds. *The Puerto Rican Diaspora: Historical Perspectives*. Philadelphia, PA: Temple University Press, pp. 1–42.

"What We Would Like to See." 1888. URL http://cdn.calisphere.org/data/13030/29/hb4t1nb029/files/hb4t1nb029FID4.jpg.

Wicherts, Jelte, Conor Dolan, and Han van der Maas. 2010. "A Systematic Literature Review of the Average IQ of Sub-Saharan Africans." *Intelligence* 38(1), pp. 1–20.

Wikipedia. 2018a. "Demographics of Puerto Rico." URL https://en.wikipedia.org/wiki/Demographics_of_Puerto_Rico.

Wikipedia. 2018b. "Economy of Puerto Rico." URL https://en.wikipedia.org/wiki/Economy_of_Puerto_Rico.

Wikipedia. 2018c. "List of Languages by Number of Native Speakers." URL https://en.wikipedia.org/wiki/List_of _languages_by_number_of_native_speakers.

Wikipedia 2018d. "List of Languages by Total Number of Speakers." URL https://en.wikipedia.org/wiki/List_of _languages_by_total_number_of_speakers.

Wikipedia 2018d. "List of Ethnic Groups in the United States by Household Income." URL https://en.wikipedia.org/wiki/ List_of_ethnic_groups_in_the_United_States_by_household_income.

Wikipedia 2018f. "Islam by Country." URL https://en.wikipedia.org/wiki/Islam_by_country.

Woetzel, Jonathan, Lenny Mendonca, Janamitra Devan, Stefano Negri, Yangmei Hu, Luke Jordan, Xiujun Li, Alexander Maasry, Geoff Tsen, Flora Yu. 2009. *Preparing for China's Urban Billion*. McKinsey Global Institute, March. URL https://www.mckinsey.com/~/media/McKinsey/Featured%20Insights/Urbanization/Preparing%20for%20 urban%20billion%20in%20China/MGI_Preparing_for_Chinas_Urban_Billion_full_report. ashx.

World Bank Group. 2016. *Poverty and Shared Prosperity 2016: Taking on Inequality*. Washington, DC: The World Bank. URL https://openknowledge.worldbank.org/bitstream/handle/10986/25078/9781464809583.pdf.

World Bank. 2018a. "China." *The World Bank*. URL https://data. worldbank.org/country/china?view=chart.

World Bank. 2018b. "GDP Deflator: United States." *The World Bank*. URL https://data.worldbank.org/indicator/NY . GDP. DEFL. ZS?locations=US.

World Bank. 2018c. "India." *The World Bank*. URL https://data.worldbank.org/country/india?view=chart.

World Bank. 2018d. "GDP per capita, PPP (current international $)." URL http: //api.worldbank.org/v2/en/indicator/NY . GDP. PCAP. PP. CD?downloadformat=excel.

World Bank. 2018e. "GDP per capita (current US$)." URL http://api.worldbank.org/v2/en/indicator/NY. GDP.PCAP . CD?downloadformat=excel.

ACKNOWLEDGMENTS

I am blessed with stellar colleagues—brilliant, cheerful, demanding, and candid. Tyler Cowen, Robin Hanson, Alex Tabarrok, and Garett Jones have enriched all my books—and *Open Borders* is no exception. Never before, however, has one of my books been blessed with a stellar coauthor. Working with Zach Weinersmith has been a daydream come true. Who would believe that a mere fanboy would get to team up with one of the world's greatest—and most thoughtful—graphic artists? Zach's ability to bring my imagination to life is nothing short of a superpower—and his soul is pure can-do sunshine. Working together has been one of my life's greatest highlights. Eternal gratitude, buddy.

I'd also like to thank the many helpful immigration researchers and activists I know, especially Michael Clemens, Shikha Dalmia, Tim Kane, Vipul Naik, Alex Nowrasteh, Lant Pritchett, Fabio Rojas, and everyone at openborders.info; GMU colleagues Nathaniel Bechhofer, Pete Boettke, Don Boudreaux, Dan Houser, Dan Klein, Steve Pearlstein, and Keller Scholl; EconLog co-bloggers David Henderson and Scott Sumner; Steven Blatt, for introducing me to graphic novels when we were students at UC Berkeley; comics guru Brian Doherty for urging me to broaden my reading; and my wife, Corina Caplan, and her parents, Corneliu and Maria Mateescu, for making me part of their family's immigration story. Our voraciously curious sons, Aidan and Tristan, have guided me every page of the way, and their younger siblings, Simon and Vali, have been hilarious sounding boards. Editors Calista Brill and Rachel Stark polished both words and pictures with great energy, Anthony Good provided above-and-beyond research assistance, and colorist Mary Cagle opened my eyes to a whole new world of hue. The Institute for Humane Studies and the Center for Study of Public Choice both provided generous financial support. Last, though we've never even talked, I owe a great intellectual debt to graphic novelists Scott McCloud and Larry Gonick. I have no idea what they think about immigration, but McCloud and Gonick showed me what graphic novels can do that mere words cannot.

—Bryan Caplan

Thank you to my wife, Kelly, who allowed me to take on this project when neither of us knew where we'd find the time, and who did well more than her fair share of housework during the sprint toward the final inks. Thanks to Bryan for roping me into this. It's rare enough in life you get to meet a favorite author, rarer that you get to work with him, and rarer still that he's as kind and intelligent as you imagined. His clear optimism even on such an uphill fight always helped me to relax as I worked. I wish to thank our editors, Calista and Rachel. Their guidance would've been welcome on any project, but with this book's sensitive topic, their suggestions were particularly valuable. I want to thank Mary Cagle, whose skill as a colorist made me look a whole lot better than I deserve to. Thanks to Lloyd James for doing some computer wizardry to make the maps look nice. I wish to thank my manager Mark Saffian for his usual guidance, and my literary agent Seth Fishman for getting us to the perfect place for this project. And I wish to thank my longtime assistant, Michael Johnson, for helping me with everything on this project from the pitch packet all the way to the website launch.

—Zach Weinersmith

First Second

Text and Art Copyright © 2019 by Bryan Douglas Caplan

Published by First Second
First Second is an imprint of Roaring Brook Press,
a division of Holtzbrinck Publishing Holdings Limited Partnership
120 Broadway, New York, NY 10271

Don't miss your next favorite book from First Second! For the latest updates go to
firstsecondnewsletter.com and sign up for our enewsletter.

Library of Congress Control Number: 2018953661
ISBN: 978-1-250-31696-7

Our books may be purchased in bulk for promotional, educational, or business use. Please contact your local
bookseller or the Macmillan Corporate and Premium Sales Department at (800) 221-7945 ext. 5442
or by email at MacmillanSpecialMarkets@macmillan.com.

First edition, 2019
Edited by Calista Brill and Rachel Stark
Book design by Andrew Arnold and Rob Steen
Colors by Mary Cagle
Color assistance by Lindsey Little, Edriel Fimbres, and Polyna Kim
Printed in Canada

Created entirely on a Wacom Cintiq, using ClipStudio.

Paperback: 10 9 8 7 6 5 4 3 2 1
Hardcover: 10 9 8 7 6 5 4 3 2 1